FAMILY RECOVERY

BUILD THE FAMILY YOU NEED
WITH THE PEOPLE YOU ALREADY HAVE

STEVE MAKOFKA

For my wife, Lorrie
You are the true originator of the content of this book.
Everything contained within it was learned with you
or from you.

For my children, Kristin, Kaitlin, Caleb and Colin
You are the exhaustive research behind this book.
I was the student, you were the teachers.

For my parents, Stan and Carol Makofka
You are the binding that holds this book together.
You are the glue and the thread behind every page.

TABLE OF CONTENTS

FOREWORD

My name is Lori and I am a person living in long-term recovery from a substance use disorder, which means that I have not had a drink or a drug for over 13 years.

This also means that my recovery from alcohol and other drugs did not prepare me for the role of being the mother of a daughter struggling with her own addiction to opiates for the better part of the last 10 years. It did not prepare me for the endless prayers to the God of my understanding to do His will for her; take her or spare her. It did not prepare me for wishing a truck would take me out so that I could escape the insanity, nor the game of convincing myself that the young lady in front of me spewing elaborate tales was not my daughter, but in fact someone I barely knew anymore.

I was not prepared to install door padlocks for rooms that contained items I did not want her steal or have access to. Nor was I prepared when she cut those same locks off to claim something of value to pawn; or to buy my own items back unless I pressed charges. I was not prepared to panic every time I saw a call coming in from her, never knowing what chaos lay ahead, or worse getting "the" call. I did not know I would now look at a group of children, playing so innocently, and think that at least one of them will battle addiction and which one was it? And I most definitely was not prepared to be a leader in the community about addiction.

My daughter and I always had a good relationship that allowed us to communicate even in her active addiction. I started asking questions and she would give the answers. Her ability to reason and articulate on the why and how of her addiction created a curious fascination into the details of the "using" culture. I was not prepared for my daughter, in active addiction, to be my biggest teacher about her addiction, and ultimately help me understand that her addiction is a chronic illness and is not controlled by poor choices. As a recovering alcoholic, I should have known that, but somehow her addiction was different than mine. Our relationship created a sense of peace for me to communicate with her and to support her in ways that helped, not hurt.

FOA was born out of the idea that families needed to be educated like I was educated, so they could feel what I felt. On a whim I started a support group with the idea that people in recovery and those that were seeking it would be welcome to attend alongside families and friends of those affected. Remember that my daughter educated me while in active addiction, therefore, complete success in recovery was not a requirement.

What started out six years ago on a whim is now a non-profit with a mission *to educate, empower and embrace families, friends and individuals struggling with addiction by providing support and promoting recovery.* FOA connects anyone touched by addiction to resources in the area by bringing in speakers. It educates and empowers by holding open discussions and sharing personal stories and experiences. A board member may have said it best, FOA is "Us helping Us".

"Us helping Us" is accurate because much of the community conversation and solutions revolve around how to provide treatment to the person addicted without much thought or concern for the family affected. Think about it. For every person in active addiction, there is most likely a minimum of four people that care about them. I realized the importance of family support and the positive impact this had person in addiction. The effect is like a waterfall, flowing from the more mature family members all the way down to the affected grandchildren; a positive ripple effect that could ultimately motivate our loved one to access treatment when ready. FOA has saved marriages, restored families, and transformed lives.

Meeting Steve Makofka was a breath of fresh air. As a person working in this space, he got it! He understood "us" and embraced that families matter and that they needed the education and support that FOA provided. Steve had the evidence-based knowledge and science that explained why a supportive family was crucial to the person in recovery. Dayton has been through a series of hardships and tragedies this past summer, and as a result, the phrase "Dayton Strong" was coined. The reality is that "we" are in our own little corner of Dayton Strong; no one is coming to save "us". Steve is in our little corner of "Us helping Us"!

It only made sense to have Steve share his knowledge at our weekly meeting. The first time Steve presented he added humor and personal experience to the topic of Thanksgiving Traditions for family and recovery. His material was simple and spot on. His firsthand stories added a dimension that created unity, trust, caring *and* laughter. This is what recovery looks like for families and anyone touched by addiction. We all know about the "How to raise healthy kids" manual that the hospital gives us the day our child is born. (*Right?*) The manual I received was missing the tab on "How to raise a child with addictions". Steve added the missing tab to my manual.

When Steve offered to create a six-part series to present during our weekly support workshops, I was excited and encouraged to have relevant content for our families delivered in a way they could relate to and implement in their own lives. This was the first time FOA had someone present a series and Steve was the perfect person to engage our members week after week. I am already looking forward to the next series!

Steve has taken the bare bones of peer content that FOA was built on, and brought order, science, descriptions to it, giving reasons for many of the family issues and situations we had discussed in the past. It has been refreshing and relieving as the facilitator and founder of FOA to have Steve on our team.

I am honored to have given Steve the platform to test the principles and insights of this book through presenting at our meetings. Families need hope and something that they can relate to and Steve delivers. As our newest FOA board member, Steve brings a candid professionalism that FOA needs for sustainable future program development. This book will be a great asset to our board and team members for years to come.

FAMILY RECOVERY: How to Build the Family you Need with the People you Already Have delivers what families and people in recovery need on the level they need it. I am encouraged that this book will be a great asset to our resource area and a guide for future open discussions.

Lori Erion, Founder of FOA Families of Addicts

AUTHOR'S NOTES

Author's Context Statement #1 Biblical References I hope the reader is not surprised, bothered, or offended by the number of Bible quotes in this book. There are a couple of reasons for them. First, I was raised in church. I am a seminary graduate, and I served as a pastor for over twenty years. It's the book I know the best and the one I have studied the most. Second, the Bible was very influential to the thinking of previous generations. Many of the concepts crucial to the understanding of the family in Western civilization are from the Bible. The concept of the Family Bible is a deep part of American tradition. For better or worse, it has had a significant impact on how we think about families. It's not my intention to change anyone's faith or religion, only to use the material I know to illustrate the principles I'm attempting to communicate.

Author's Context Statement #2 The Value of Life
In the writing of this book, I have tried to be both Pro-Life and Pro-Choice. Life has value, and people have the freedom and responsibility to make choices. I present myself as a traditional, conservative, theistic humanist. I believe there is something greater than us who we can call God. I also believe all human lives have intrinsic value and equal worth due to the fact that they are human and have life.

Author's Context Statement #3 ACT Therapy

Many of the concepts in this book are borrowed from ACT Therapy. The book is intended to be ACT Therapy compatible. Those who are familiar with ACT Therapy will find the six core principles woven throughout the text. These core principles are mindfulness, self-as-context, acceptance, defusion, values, and action.

Author's Context Statement #4 Sex and Gender

The goal of this book is to be as universal and timeless as possible. It is also meant to be a practical tool anyone can use to help themselves build a strong, healthy, supportive family. Obviously, sex and gender are essential parts of how we understand family. My goal in writing this book is to be as open and inclusive as possible. I want to focus on the things that are agreed on, not the issues disputed. My goal is also to state family principles and behaviors in positive terms—as in, what we are in favor of and things we can do—not in negative terms—as in, what we are against and things we don't do. Conflict is a normal part of family and discussions about family. My goal is to decrease the conflict, not increase it.

INTRODUCTION

I want to open your mind to a big idea. The big idea is this. Everybody deserves a strong, healthy, supportive family. That sounds basic. But I want you to stop and think about it. Think about the word, *everybody*.

If you are oppositional and you like to argue, you might want to say, "Certainly, there's somebody who doesn't deserve a strong, healthy, supportive family." You may know that person. You may think of someone you don't like or someone who has done some really horrible things. Maybe that person who hurt you or stole from you. But I'm going to try to change the way you think about it.

Everybody deserves a strong, heathy, supportive family. People who have done bad things, people who have made mistakes, people who don't come from good families. There are no exceptions. The foundational thought that I want to put into place is that everybody deserves a strong, healthy, supportive family.

Now, if that statement is true, then this second statement is also true. You deserve a strong, healthy, supportive family. It may take some effort to open up some space in your brain for that thought. But I want you to do it. I want you to let it in. You deserve a strong, healthy, supportive family. Now, you may have some negative thoughts associated with that. You may think some of the following things:

- You don't know me.

- You don't know where I've been.

- You don't know who I am.

- You don't know what I've done.

- You don't know some of the things I've said.

- You don't know where I've come from.

- You don't know all the mistakes I've made.

- I don't deserve a strong, healthy, supportive family.

Or maybe you're thinking:

- You don't know my family.

- You don't know the family I came from.

- You don't know the family I have.

- You don't know the things that have happened in my family.

- If I ever deserved a strong, healthy, supportive family, I don't anymore.

I want you to let those negative thoughts go and embrace this idea. It's okay if you have a strong, healthy, and support-ive family. I want you to say it with me. I deserve a strong, healthy, supportive family. This is the participation part of the process. I want you to be actively engaged in the material.

So, how do you build a family? It's easy, right? Fall in love. Get married. Have kids. Boom. You've got a normal family.

But how normal is that pattern? Is that how it has worked in your family? If you look back over three generations, how many exceptions are there to the rule? I grew up in that normal-pattern kind of family. Or at least as a child, I thought I did. But when I got older, I found out my parents didn't exactly follow it. Some of their parents didn't follow it. And some of my kids haven't followed it.

The reality of what constitutes a family has undergone significant changes in my lifetime. The percentage of children growing up in two parent homes has gone from 87% in 1960 to 69% in 2014. The percentage of those parents still in their first marriage has dropped from 73% to 46%. The number of one-parent homes has increased from 9% (less than 1 out of 10) to 26% (more than 1 out of 4).[1] Those are some significant changes.

When you stop and think about it, human life is all about family. Every part of life has a family dimension. It is also marked by family influence. I believe everyone wants a strong, healthy, supportive family. And I believe everyone deserves one.

For the last five years I have been an educator on an adolescent psych inpatient unit. I can't think of a single issue we have dealt with that didn't have a family dimension to it. I hear them say, "I just want my parents to understand and be supportive." My wife and I watch *The Voice*. Who is it that's usually standing right offstage giving support? Family. Who is it that motivates the singer to take the risk and perform? Family. Who is it that rushes onstage and shares the celebration or the rejection? Family.

If you listen to an acceptance speech in almost any setting, you will probably hear a family reference. Either the support of a family member was crucial to their success, or the lack of support from family was an obstacle they had to overcome or the emotional pain they had to endure. Either way, acknowledging family is frequently a part of their speech.

Family support is a pretty reliable predictor of success. James S. Coleman first documented it in his 1966 "Study of Equality of Educational Opportunity." And recently, even the Huffington Post said, "If you want to raise a child who is caring, organized, goal oriented, and successful, you must provide a stable environment in which (they) can experience a childhood filled with both love and bonding experiences." [2]

If building a strong, healthy, successful family is that important, where can you get reliable information on how to build one?

There are three kinds of experts on raising families.

The first kind is people who have no children of their own. They know exactly what you should be doing with your children and are often quite free with their unsolicited advice.

The second kind is those who have already raised their children. Parents who are still in the process of raising their children know they are not experts and hang on for dear life hoping for the best. These parents have some perspective on what they did right and what they wish they had done differently.

The third kind of expert are those with impressive academic credentials who write the books that are read by the first two other kinds of experts.

My wife and I are the second kind of experts. We both have advanced degrees, but mostly, we have experience. Our four children are close enough in age that for a short period, they were *all* teenagers at the same time. Those were interesting years. Alcohol, drug abuse, boyfriends, girlfriends, sibling fights, seizures, car accidents, 3:00 am phone calls, court, jail, self-harm, depression, teen pregnancy. When I was discussing the idea for writing this book, a friend told me, "I wish I had your book when I was raising my kids." My response was, "I wish I had my book when I was raising *my* kids."

Lorrie and I come from very different families. Both our families have issues. A lot of issues. But the one thing both our families have in common is that they are very supportive.

We are who we are because of the support we have received from our families, and we are attempting to pass that legacy on to our children and grandchildren.

As of the writing of this book, my parents live around the corner from me. They are a short five-minute walk away. My oldest daughter and her family are a ten-minute drive away while my second daughter lives twenty minutes away in the next town over. Up until recently one son lived with us, he now has an apartment a few blocks away. The youngest son lives in Chicago. On Lorrie's side of the family, her brother and his family live three hours away. Her mother and her other brother live across the street from them. We understand the whole multigenerational thing. My wife and I are a part of what some people refer to it as the sandwich generation—the ones in the middle caring for both parents and children. More specifically, we are part of the club-sandwich group. There are four layers. Four generations. We have parents, each other, kids, and grandkids involved in our lives. It's great.

We've also helped others all our lives. In the late 1980s, we started as inner-city pastors in Philadelphia. I served in multiple churches as a youth pastor and senior pastor. In 2013, I started working on a mental health inpatient unit, teaching life skills to both adolescents and adults. Lorrie delivered babies as a labor and delivery nurse for thirty-five years, following in her mother's footsteps. Like the ad from Farmers Insurance says, "We know a thing or two because we've seen a thing or two." (cue the music: "We are Farmers. Bum ba dum bum; bum bum bum.") In 2018, I received my certification as a Family Life Educator from the National Council on Family Relations. NCFR is made up of the people who do the research on how families actually work. They are professors and clinicians from across the country. I share my own stories and experiences, but I also check to make sure the principles in this book are backed up by the latest studies and research.

My goal is to help you build your family. You may come from a strong, healthy, supportive family, or your family roots may be withered and twisted. You may have embraced the heritage you received from your parents, or you may be trying to break dysfunctional family patterns that have existed for generations. One thing I know for sure—

I know it's possible because my parents did it. The family I grew up in was much different than the families my parents grew up in. And the family that my kids grew up in was different than the home I grew up in.

> IT IS POSSIBLE TO CHANGE YOUR FAMILY TREE IN ONE BRANCH.

I am grateful for the help and support of my friends in Families of Addicts. In 2013, Dayton, Ohio, was at the epicenter of the nation's opioid addiction crisis. Families of Addicts was formed by Lori Erion to work with not only the addicts themselves but also with their families. Many of the principles and insights in this book were first presented at their meetings.

I also want to thank all of the members of the National Council on Family Relations. Their thoughts, research, and influence are woven through the fabric of this book. When I first started on this journey of working with families, they helped me unpack the essential concepts and gave me direction. I wouldn't have made it this far without them.

A strong, healthy, supportive family can be one of the closest things to heaven on earth. And a hurtful, dysfunctional family can be one of the closest things to hell on earth. The good individuals our society needs to function and survive are best produced in strong, healthy, supportive families. For all our sakes, let's get to work.

PART I

WHAT IS A
SUPPORTIVE
FAMILY?

1

WHAT IS A FAMILY?

Let's start with the basics. What do what I mean by "family?" Words have a range of meaning. What I mean by family may not be what you mean by family. If I asked you to picture your family who are the people that you're going to picture.

All families are complicated if you look below the surface. If you want to learn about complicated families, read the Bible. Or study Greek mythology. Or watch a movie. *Any* Marvel or DC character—Batman, Superman, Guardians of the Galaxy, Black Panther, Wonder Woman—all have family issues. Yes, it's complicated.

What is a family?

Words are funny things. Different people use the same word at different times to convey different ideas. If we are going to have a productive conversation about family, it will be helpful if we all use the same word in the same way to communicate the same thought. To do that, let's sharpen our focus and clarify some terms. One way to do that is to clarify what we are not talking about. Let's look at some things that family is not.

1. HAVING RELATIVES IS NOT THE SAME AS HAVING A FAMILY.

Some people refer to their relatives as kin. The older, technical definition of family was "related by blood or law." If you were physically related, you were family. By law, you could add family members by marriage or adoption. Hospitals used to have visitation policies designed for family members only. But those policies sometimes kept supportive people out and allowed troublesome people in.

Let's be realistic.

NOT ALL RELATIVES ARE FAMILY.

Some relatives are distant. It's not necessarily bad, and it's nobody's fault, but you are far away from them. Sometimes geographically, sometimes relationally. You probably have distant relatives you haven't seen for a while. You don't really know anything about them. They're not really a part of your life. You are barely aware they exist.

In fact, you may have relatives you don't even know about. When my mother-in-law was in her sixties, she got a phone message from a lady saying, "You don't know me, but I'm your sister. Would you like to get together?" In my family, there are all sorts of uncles, aunts, nieces, and nephews who have never met. Are they related? Yes. Do they function as family? No.

I always smile when I hear businesses use family language in their advertising. "Come on in," they say. "We'll treat you like family." Depending on your family background, that may be attractive or downright terrifying. Imagine that you go out to eat at a restaurant that features family-style dining. Now, imagine the family style they have in mind is the family you grew up in. What does that dining experience look like?

NOT ALL FAMILY ARE RELATIVES.

There are a lot of ways people you are not related become family. Sometimes your child has a friend who s more time at your house than they do at their own, and they become family. Sometimes the regulars at bars and clubs are so close they function as family. In Dayton, Ohio, one of my favorite places to hang out is the Yellow Cab Tavern. It's a home-away-from-home for me. The people there have met many of my relatives. It's where I did the release party for my kid's album. The poster for that accomplishment is hanging on the wall behind the bar. It feels like home. It feels like family.

YOU CAN HAVE PEOPLE WHO ARE BOTH RELATIVES AND FAMILY.

These are very strong ties, and you should be grateful for them. Just because we are making a distinction between the two terms doesn't mean they can't overlap. There is a comfort, strength, and support you get from people you are related to. You've known them, and they've known you for your entire life. They show up to give love and support.

My granddaughter is an Irish dancer, and she recently danced on stage at our local theatre. In the audience that night were one set of grandparents, one great-grandpa, two great-grandmas, and a great-aunt who happened to be in town. That kind of family support makes you dance better.

2. HAVING A PEER GROUP IS NOT THE SAME AS HAVING A FAMILY.

A peer group is made up of ... well ... peers. Peers are people about your same age. They are people you like and agree with and you have a lot of things in common. Family may be none of those things. Peer groups can be very support-ive, but because they lack diversity, they can be very limited in perspective. Peer groups can model some of the traits of a family, but they don't function well as a substitute for it.

Dynamic families have a multigenerational perspective. This is generally a healthy thing, but it can also be a source of friction. We live in an age of increased polarization, and some of that growing tension is generational. But generational conflict is not a new thing.

Historians generally believe the naming of generations began in the 20th century. **Gertrude Stein** is considered the first to have done so. She bestowed the title of Lost Generation on those who had been born around the turn of the century and bore the brunt of service during World War I. In the epigram to Ernest Hemingway's *The Sun Also Rises*, published in 1926, Stein wrote, "You are all a lost generation." [1]

However, if we look a little deeper, we discover that generational conflict is as old as recorded history. Even the Bible is full of generational descriptions and conflict. Hebrew culture kept records of generations. We call them genealogies. Many of the readers of this book have probably done some research on their own genealogies. When the Gospel of Matthew talks about Jesus, it gives a great deal of attention to his genealogy. It makes a point that "from Abraham to David, were fourteen generations, fourteen generations from David to the deportation; and from the deportation to Babylon to the Messiah, fourteen generations." (Matthew 1:17)

One of the most significant descriptions of generational differences and conflict is found in the book of Judges. Three generations are described. There was the first generation that grew up as slaves in Egypt. There was a second generation that grew up wandering in the wilderness. And there was a third generation that was born in the Promised Land who "did not know the Lord or the works of the Lord." (Judges 2:10)

Why do I bring the Bible into this? To demonstrate that generational conflict is not new. Each generation's perspective is shaped by their shared experiences. That may be World War I, the Great Depression, Pearl Harbor, the assassination of

John F. Kennedy, Columbine, 9-11, or the 2016 presidential election.

I find it ironic to hear members of the Baby Boomer generation criticize Millennials for not respecting their elders. Really? Which generation was it that said, "Don't trust anyone over thirty?" And they said it when they were in their late twenties. That wasn't very far-sighted.

Every generation has areas of clarity, and every generation has blind spots. This is normal. Intergenerational conflict is normal, and in many cases, it is healthy. Proverbs 20:29 says that "the glory of youth is their strength, and the glory of the old is their gray hair." The value of young people is their strength, energy, new perspective and ability to change things that need to be changed. The value of older people is in their wisdom, experience, and the ability to preserve things of value.

One of the favorite expressions of generational conflict I've ever heard was from the film Nobody's Fool. The son says, "I would hope by the time I'm your age, I'm a little smarter than that." The father says, "Can't hurt to hope. You sure are off to a slow start."

It is very difficult to learn respect for others from within a peer group. The tighter and more homogenous the peer group, the less respect it tends to have for others outside the group. Respect is learned in diverse, multigenerational settings. Children are to learn respect for others. Adolescents have to develop self-respect. Adults gain or lose respect by their choices, behaviors, and accomplishments. Elders receive respect and leverage it for the benefit of the family.

3. HAVING PETS IS NOT THE SAME AS HAVING A FAMILY.

I know some readers aren't going to like this, but I think it needs to be said. I love animals. In my lifetime, I have had ducks, chickens, a pony, sheep, goats, seven dogs, three cats, fish, turtles, hamsters, gerbils, guinea pigs, rabbits, and a chinchilla as pets. Dogs, cats, and other animals can be a wonderful part of your family. But if your family is *only* made up of non-human members, you have a problem. Your golden retriever may love you unconditionally, but he's not going to drive you to the hospital, and you can't give him power of attorney. Animals and pets can be a wonderful part of a dynamic family, but at least *some* of your family has to be made up of other humans. Even if you grew up in the jungle and were raised by apes or wolves, some day you are going to need to connect with other humans.

4. HAVING ONLINE CONTACTS IS NOT THE SAME AS HAVING A FAMILY.

I believe we live in the greatest age of technology that has ever existed. Smart phones and laptops are amazing devices that can add quality and value to important relationships. One recent study even indicated that "meeting online leads to happier, more enduring marriages."[3] Online interactions can enhance healthy relationships, but they cannot be a substitute for real, live, face to face, in person interactions. As Groucho Marx once said, "I'm not crazy about reality, but it's still the only place to get a decent meal." He said that way before the Internet and virtual reality existed, and he's still right. Eating alone all the time isn't fun. Sometimes you want to share a meal with others.

If that's what family is not, then how do we define what family is?

I'm going to start off with a very simple definition. A family is a network of relationships.

It's a simple definition, but when it comes to families, things don't stay simple very long. In fact, they can get very complicated very quickly. Why?

THERE IS AN ELEMENT OF CHOICE IN FAMILY RELATIONSHIPS.

The older you get, the more choice you have in who you consider to be family. In the background of most cultures and societies, there is an element of choice when it comes to family members. There is a recognition that someone can function as family without meeting the technical qualifications of blood and law. Rituals are established for adopting or accepting someone as a family member. Sometimes there are rituals for disowning a family member, such as writing them out of the will.

In the Christian tradition, there is a long history of recognizing the concept of spiritual family—Jesus himself opened the door to this idea. When told that his mother and brothers were waiting for him, he replied, "'Who is my mother, and who are my brothers?' Pointing to his disciples, he said, 'Here are my mother and my brothers. For whoever does the will of my Father in heaven is my brother and sister and mother.'" (Matthew 12:48-50) Jesus also indicated that while honoring father and mother was an important part of the law, there were other principles that could supersede loyalty to biological family. He said, "If anyone comes to me and does not hate father and mother, wife and children, brothers and sisters—yes, even their own life—such a person cannot be my disciple." (Luke 14:26) The meaning and application of this verse are fiercely debated within the Christian community. My own interpretation is that in this context, the word *hate* should be interpreted as "a willingness to disregard" rather than "a desire to harm."

The church I grew up in was quite willing to refer to non-family members as brother or sister. Adults in this extended church family, were often referred to as uncle or aunt. We embraced the idea that church was a family based on shared spiritual values and relationships rather than blood and law.

One of my favorite movie scenes is from *Remember the Titans*. Gary, the team Superman, is lying in a hospital bed, partially paralyzed after a car accident. His friend Julius comes in to visit him. Gary is white; Julius is black. The nurse interrupts them and tells Julius he has to leave. "Only kin's allowed in here," she explains. Gary protests, "Alice, are you blind? Can't you see the family resemblance? That's my brother." There are also what I call Fast and Furious" families. In the movie series, all sorts of behaviors are justified by saying, "Yeah, it's family." The word is used 33 times in the franchise.[2]

FAMILY STATUS IS SOMETHING THAT CAN BE GIVEN.

The idea is that it is given for life. Wedding vows usually include "till death do us part." Acknowledging someone as family is a big deal, especially when it's communicated. I will always remember my granddaughter's adoption ceremony. Her step-dad wanted to make it official. The judge called her up on the platform and interviewed her, then he gave her a mini keepsake gavel that she used to make it official. There were hugs and tears and a lot of pictures.

IT IS POSSIBLE TO HAVE MULTIPLE FAMILIES

I'm not talking about the times when Daddy traveled a lot and had another wife and a kid in a different town. I'm talking about the idea that you can have different kinds of families. I learned this from listening to a man in recovery. He was expressing gratitude and thanking people who contributed to his success. He said, "I thank God, my family, my church family, my recovery family, my family at FOA (Families of Addicts) and my work family." That's five different families. And they all served different functions at different times. When people and groups function as family, they become family. They should be granted family status.

What happens when you grant family status to someone you are not biologically related to? What are you saying? What constitutes a family tie? Family is a group of people who have a durable bond. They have something significant in common. There is a level of commitment to each other. The relationship is not primarily based on emotion. Can you create the network you need with the people you have? Yes. Church can become family. Work can become family. Band members and team mates can become family. Or your actual biological family can become your support family. We are taking about a very functional approach to family.

"How your family works is more important than how it looks."

2

WHO IS MY FAMILY?

When it comes to identifying family members, how do you know who is part of your family?

There are five essential traits of a strong, healthy, supportive family. These are the traits that make a group of people feel like a family. When they are present, the group feels like family. If they are absent or weak, the group won't feel like a family, even if everybody in the group is related to each other.

These five traits are—

1. Belonging

2. Acceptance

3. Sharing

4. Support

5. Time

Let's look at them individually.

1. BELONGING—FAMILIES PRODUCE A SENSE OF BELONGING.

It is my belief that family is the first social unit to nurture a sense of belonging. Family is our sense of roots, our orientation for where we have come from and whether we are making progress or going backward. This may be because of our biological roots. It may also be because of our geographical roots.

A sense of belonging tends to develop when a "person experiences being valued, needed, or important with respect to others" and "when the person experiences a fit or congruence with other people." [1] If you grew up in a family where you weren't valued, needed, or made to feel important, you will probably struggle with a sense of belonging for your entire life. The same is true if you grew up in a family where you didn't feel like you fit in.

It's difficult for people who don't have a sense of belonging to feel settled. As expressed in the song, "Corner of the Sky," from the musical, *Pippin*,

> Cats fit on the windowsill
> Children fit in the show
> Why do I feel I don't fit in
> Anywhere I go.[2]

Belonging also includes a sense of ownership and a sense of membership. It's a mutual ownership: I'm yours, and you're mine. We belong together. We belong to each other. Membership includes acceptance of certain rights and responsibilities. To be a member of a group means simply to be recognized as a functioning part. Like the American Express ad says, "Membership has its privileges."

2. ACCEPTANCE—FAMILIES OFFER UNCONDITIONAL ACCEPTANCE

Home is the place where, when you have to go there,
they have to take you in.

—Robert Frost

Now, let me clarify what I mean by unconditional acceptance. To have a strong, healthy, supportive family, you must know the difference between accepting a person and accepting their behavior. These are two different things. You can accept a person and tell them, "I love you, and you're family, but what you just did … that behavior … is not okay. It is not acceptable."

In mental health and recovery circles, we talk a lot about boundaries. Acceptance is when boundaries are respected and recognized but crossing them does not threaten the relationship. Like when a non-smoking family member hosts a family event. The family members who smoke are accepted and welcome to come, but they're not allowed to smoke inside. If they want to smoke, they have to do it out on the back porch. Families relationships are strong relationships. They survive hardship and conflict. They have the ability to say, "I accept you, even when I can't accept your behavior."

Unconditional acceptance is hard to find and difficult to maintain, but it is an essential part of what makes family relationships special. To practice unconditional acceptance, you have to distinguish between the person, the relationship, and the behavior. Unconditional acceptance means that the person is accepted because of who they are. It's based on their status as a family member, but it doesn't mean everything they do is acceptable. The nature of the relationship can be changed by unacceptable behavior, but the relationship itself isn't threatened by the other person's behavior.

In a family setting, relationships are based on something other than emotion. The emotion in the relationship can fluctuate wildly, yet it won't jeopardize the relationship itself. It's expressed in the sentence, "You're still my child, and I still love you, but I am not happy with you right now." We will explore this aspect of family relationships more fully in Chapter 11 and describe what it looks like in action.

Accepting a person unconditionally comes at a great cost. To love someone for who they are, you have to let go of your expectations of them. You have to let go of who you think they *should* be. You have to let go of who you think they *could* be. You have to be able to love who they are *at this point in time*. Loving someone for their potential can be a bad idea. You have to love the person for who they are, not for who they have the potential of becoming. As a musician, I've been to my share of tryouts and auditions. One of the most common responses musicians get in auditions is "you have a lot of potential." What you learn over time is what that really means. "You have lots of potential" really means "you're not good enough yet."

I believe one of my gifts is the ability to see potential in people. But loving someone for who they could be, not for who they are, is actually a form of rejection. It's not loving them, it's loving a person who doesn't yet exist. I am grateful my wife was able to see the potential that was in me and encourage it. But she was also able to love me for who I was, not only for who I could become.

Carl Jung said, "The greatest burden a child must bear is the unlived life of its parents." But it may also be true that the greatest burden a parent must bear may be the unlived life of the child. Every child comes with a set of hopes, dreams, and expectations. No child ever exactly matches the ideals of their parents. The parent must be willing to let go of the child they wanted and love the child they have. Unplanned events like addictions and teen pregnancies can change a child's future instantly. With family, the unconditional acceptance of the person is based on the pre-existing family relationship, not the ability of the person to meet the expectations of another family member.

But let me say it again. Just because a family offers unconditional acceptance of the person, it doesn't mean the family is able to unconditionally accept any and all behaviors from that person. Learning how to behave and act with other people is one of the primary functions of a family.

In a healthy family, you have the freedom to be whoever you are, but that does not give you the freedom to do whatever you want.

The other members of the family have the freedom to respond however they want and set boundaries they feel are appropriate.

3. SUPPORT—FAMILIES CONSIST OF SUPPORTIVE RELATIONSHIPS

Just as being accepting of a person doesn't mean you accept any and all of their behavior, being supportive of a person doesn't mean you support every decision they make.

Supporting the person means you want them to succeed. Supporting the person means you want them to be happy. However, sometimes supporting a person means *not* supporting a particular decision they've made.

If we truly believe a family member is about to marry the wrong person, love obligates us to at least express our concerns. But family support will obligate us to show up at the wedding. If the marriage goes well, we support the couple's success. If it ends badly, we show up to help ease the pain and help with the healing process. Whether we articulate the "I tried to tell you" idea depends on the person and the relationship.

In Families in Addicts, they use the phrase "We will help you live, but we will not help you die." If the other person is going down a road of self-destruction, we can't go with them, and we can't support them on that road. But at the point where they want to make good choices, we support them and their decisions.

Support is essential to a healthy family. Being supportive means you have committed yourself to someone else's success. Because you are tied together by a family relationship, you are tied to helping them succeed. You are invested in their happiness and success. This doesn't mean you automatically rescue them from the consequences of their own behavior. It means that when you allow them to suffer the negative consequences of their own choices and behavior, you are not doing so out of anger, jealousy, or vengeance, but out of love. You are not interfering because you know that doing so would not be beneficial for you or them. Furthermore, you know that enabling them will only encourage the negative patterns and perhaps feed into your own codependence.

How do you know who is on your team or in your family? Look for those who are rooting for your success.

4. SHARING—FAMILIES ARE DEVELOPED BY SHARING GOOD AND BAD EXPERIENCES.

Rejoice with those who rejoice. Weep with those who weep.

—Romans 12:15

Part of what makes family special is shared experiences, both good and bad. When you have been through a lot together, it tends to draw you close. Sharing experiences strengthens and develops relationships. Even though sharing heritage can be enough to begin a family relationship, feeling like family still requires you to share experiences. It's expressed in sentences that begin with the words, "Remember that time when we ..."

In a healthy family, there should be a balance of both positive and negative shared experiences. But what happens when the experiences are mostly—if not entirely—negative? Do we still hold on to those relationships as family? With biological family, there is a greater tolerance for negative shared experiences. There can be an imbalance, and the relationship can be maintained because of the biological component. Voluntary family relationships have less tolerance for a negative experience imbalance. If you are in a voluntary family relationship that is predominantly or entirely made up of negative experiences, it may be an indication that it is a toxic relationship. Efforts can be made to make it into a healthy relationship, but it is possible that the relationship may have to be discontinued in the interest of self-preservation. In other words, you may have to let go of it.

5. TIME—FAMILIES TAKE TIME TO DEVELOP.

Families take time. It takes time to build them, and it takes time to maintain them.

In the biological realm, it's possible to conceive of an instant family (pun intended), but it still takes nine months to develop. Two people meet, have sex, get pregnant, give birth, and voila, instant bio-family. This was the plot line explored in the 2007 movie, *Knocked Up*. But would these people be able to take their situation and make a strong, healthy, supportive family out of it? (It's a romantic comedy. What do you think?)

In 2018, Mark Walhberg released a movie called *Instant Family*. It was based on the true story of a family that took in three foster children. In one decision, a childless couple became parents of three children. The point of the movie was that it took time to add all the ingredients that eventually made them a family.

How long does it take for voluntary relationships to take on the aspects of family? In the case of an exceptional, dramatic event, it can happen quite quickly. But generally, the relationship has to survive some changes before it starts to take on the character of a family relationship. It may take more than one life stage, relationships that extend from adolescent to adulthood, or from adulthood to old age.

When a relationship outlasts the circumstances that created it, it tends to feel like family. For instance, say you form a relationship with someone who is part of a work context, and the relationship becomes a friendship that goes beyond the co-worker context. Then one or both of you change jobs, but the friendship continues. Then one of you experiences a significant life-changing event, and the relationship endures. Now, it's starting to feel like family.

A note to step-parents: Give it time. Marriage and adoption can change the legal status of a relationship, but it takes time to change the nature of a relationship.

3

WHY DO FAMILIES EXIST?

To understand why families are necessary, it's helpful to step back and look at them from the perspective of an entire lifespan. Below is a chart of life stages (from: Family Life Education: The Practice of Family Science)[1]

Think for a moment about how each life stage would be affected by the words, *no family*. Picture a woman who recently found out she is pregnant, and she has no family. A baby is carried into a hospital by a first provider who says to the nurse, "He doesn't have a family." In the *no family* column, I put a word that comes to mind when I think of being in that life stage and having no family. In the next column I put in a word that describes the person with a supportive family. It's not scientific, but it creates an image of the difference that having a supportive family can make.

Life Stage	No Family	With Family
Prenatal	Vulnerable	Safe
Infancy/Toddler, birth -2	Tragic	Nurtured
Early Childhood, 3-5	Abandoned	Guided
Middle/Late Childhood, 6-11	Confused	Blossoming
Adolescence, 12-18	Lost	Protected
Emerging Adulthood, 19-25	Wandering	Rooted
Early Adulthood, 26-38	Alienated	Connected
Middle Adulthood, 40-65	Empty	Rewarded
Late Adulthood, 65 and up	Lonely	Honored
End of Life	Sad	Legacy

How is each life stage different when it is experienced in the context of a strong, healthy, supportive family? There are so many words that can be used, but I think we can all agree it's better. A strong, healthy, supportive family makes every stage of life better. As you look at your current life stage and look back at previous life stages, how has the presence or absence of family affected that experience?

At any life stage, when a patient arrives at a hospital for physical or mental health reasons, one of the first questions that is asked is "do they have any family?" In the cases of early and late life stages, one of the first priorities in treatment is to find some way to put together a support network for them, to build some kind of family out of the people they have.

Why are families necessary? What are they supposed to provide?

1. SURVIVAL

Safety, survival, food, clothing, and shelter. These are our basic needs. And from the beginning of human history, it's been easier to acquire them if you are a part of a family. Americans are notoriously individualistic. We come by it honestly. We act as if the individual is the basic unit of society. This is not true of most other cultures and hasn't been true for most of human history.

In every stage of human history, involvement in a family unit increased your likelihood of survival. Hunter/gatherer society? Family helps. Agrarian society? Family helps. Industrial society? Family helps. Twenty-first century digital information age? Guess what? There are increasing numbers of young adults living at home with their parents. Two or more incomes may be needed to afford food and housing. Family helps.

Baby humans take a long time develop. Most mammals take a year or two at the most until they can go off and fend for themselves. Baby humans take much longer—somewhere between twelve to thirty years. We are designed to need the support of a family. Life is a team sport. Family is your first team. I have talked with suicidal teens on the inpatient unit who described their parents' reaction as "absolutely freaked out." I have asked them, "Do you want to know why your parents freaked out? I'll tell you why. You made them face their worst fear. Parents are supposed to be motivated by love. But most of the time they are motivated by fear. Parents are basically just holding on and scared to death. And there's one fear in particular that parents have. The one that keeps them awake at night. Do you know what it is? The fear is having to go to your funeral."

That is a wound that doesn't heal.

2. SENSE OF SELF—PERSONAL DEVELOPMENT

Families are critical for knowing who you are as a person. What you know and believe about yourself was probably formed in your family context. If you grew up with a strong, healthy, supportive family who thought you were wonderful, who equipped you for life, where you knew you were loved and cared for, who helped you succeed, then you probably have all of that inside of you.

But, if you grew up in a family that didn't give you that … a family that told you you're a loser … you're a mistake …

you're worthless ... you ruined our lives, all those messages that you got early are now part of your thinking and part of your identity. Part of the function of family is to let us know who we are and to help us have a healthy self-image. Are we good at everything? No. Are we bad at everything? No. We all have strengths and weaknesses. We have meaning. We have purpose. We have direction. These are the things a family context is supposed to provide for you—a sense of self, knowing who you are and being okay with it.

It's very hard to know who you are without knowing where you came from. One of the most common themes in heroic literature is the story of the child who is raised by someone other than their parents. Their identity is hidden from them until later in life. Then as an adolescent or young adult, they meet someone who knows who they really are, who knows who their parents were. And now, with this new identity, they must begin their quest and embrace their destiny. The hero announces their newfound identity as, "I am _____, child of _____." They know who they are because they know where they came from.

For the purposes of family studies, both your genetics and your environment are related to your family identity. We will get more into the stages of family development in the next chapter. But you are who you are because of your family. The way you think, feel how you feel, why you do what you do, is because of family influences. Yes, there are other influences such as teachers, coaches, schools, neighbors, and friends. But even the exposure to these people is a result of family influences.

If we want to develop better human beings, we need to develop better families. If we want to know who we are as individuals, we need to develop strong, healthy, supportive families. If we want a healthy level of self-love, self-respect, and self-esteem, we need to make peace with our family history and the people involved in it.

3. SENSE OF OTHERS—SOCIAL DEVELOPMENT

Family is where we are supposed to learn how to behave around others. Where are you supposed to learn how to share? Where are you supposed to learn how to respond to the word, *no*? Where are you supposed to learn how to respect other people's boundaries, authority, responsibility, and all the things that we need to get along together? Answering these questions is a primary function of family. If the family you grew up in was lacking in this area, it's not surprising that when you get with a group of people, you have no idea who you are and no idea how to act around others.

It used to be called upbringing. As in, "He ain't got no upbringing. He don't know better." That's a family issue. In his book, *Hillbilly Elegy*, J.D. Vance talks about the struggles of transitioning from the mountain culture of his youth to the more sophisticated culture where he received his education. Fortunately, a mentor helped him adapt to his new culture. He had to learn when to sit, when to stand, what to say, and which fork to use.

Learning concepts like sharing with our peers, responding to authority, respecting other people's boundaries and opinions should be part of family upbringing. Yes, these concepts can be taught in non-family settings like school and day care. But ask any teacher you know if family upbringing makes a difference. Ask about the conflict, tension, and anxiety kids feel when the values they are taught at school aren't reinforced at home.

FAMILY AND SOCIETY

Allow me to get slightly political for a moment. Another part of socialization is knowing how to act in a free, democratic society. "Democracies require a certain kind of citizen to survive. The ability to self-regulate precedes the ability to self-govern. As John Adams so famously said, "Our Constitution was made only for a moral and religious people.

It is wholly inadequate to the government of any other." The US Citizenship and Immigration Services website says, "We are a nation bound not by race or religion, but by the shared values of freedom, liberty, and equality." Where are those shared values passed on to the next generation? In families. If we want to live in a better world, we are going to need to be the kind of people who can produce and maintain it. Better citizens, if you will. And the best way to produce better citizens is to work to create better families.

DIFFERENTIATION

Given the fact that our families may or may not have done a good job at providing the essentials for us, how should we relate to them now?

One of the key concepts in understanding how families work is the idea of differentiation. Differentiation is the observation that we first learn who we are in the context of family. We develop an identity and role as *part of* the family. Then later in life, we have to differentiate ourselves from our family context. We have to learn who we are *apart from* our family.

When I worked on an adolescent inpatient unit, we would frequently admit have children who didn't have the ability, or did not know how to behave in socially appropriate ways. Our inpatient unit was a safe, structured, respect-based environment. We tried to make it feel like family.

Once the kids realized they were safe and respected, they would often modify their behavior and respond to us in more appropriate ways. Many of the disrespectful, self-destructive behaviors they displayed were actually self-protective and were developed in their home and family context. When the context changed, the behavior changed, and they evolved more into the person they wanted to be.

That is, until the parents showed up for visitation. Then they would revert back to their old behaviors or what we called "beast mode." It was a differentiation issue. They had learned to be one person at home, but they had the ability and desire to be a better person when around others.

This is part of the reason why kids act one way at home and another way at school. It is also the same reason grown adults will act one way with their spouse and children but revert to younger behavior when they interact with their own parents. Family relations work better when the individual has a strong sense of who they are apart from the family and can then bring that identity back into their family of origin.

LIFE IS A TEAM SPORT

And your family is your first team. You can't consistently win in a team sport by yourself. Just ask Lebron James (Ohio humor). You can't survive in life without a team. In primitive times, if you had to take down a woolly mammoth to eat and survive, you were more likely to succeed if you had a team, tribe, or clan to help. In later times, if you were running a farm, it helped to have a strong partner and a lot of kids to plow the fields and care for the livestock. Now, if you are trying to survive on a minimum wage job and keep a roof over your head, it's best to have a team.

Let me explain what I mean by "life is a team sport." In team sports, when it's your turn, you have to step up and do your thing. You perform as an individual, but you compete and train as a team. Swimmers, golfers, gymnastics, wrestlers, track and field, all identify as a team, but they perform as individuals. You can win your event, and your team can lose. You can lose your event, and your team can win. You have the responsibility to do your best and contribute to the team. It's about you, but it's not *all* about you.

Consider more traditional team sports like baseball, football, soccer, basketball, and volleyball. In these sports, you have to focus on playing your position. In baseball, you have to step up to the plate. Do you know what happens to the batter most of the time when they step up to the plate? They get out and walk back to the dugout. In baseball, if you get a hit one out of three times, you are a superstar. In basketball, if you only miss half your shots, you are a good player. It's not about being perfect. It's about functioning as part of a team. Good teams defeat good players. Good teams make good players better. Everyone wants their family to be a good team.

When it comes to family, though, some of you may feel like a first-round-pick quarterback who got drafted by the Cleveland Browns (more Ohio humor). You know you're a good player, but your team has a long history of losing (Cleveland Browns, 2017, 0-16). You want to be on a good team, but you didn't get to choose your family or your place in it. Now, what do you do?

Start building your own team or try to join a new team.

THE THREE STAGES OF FAMILY DEVELOPMENT

there are three different stages of family development that we have to consider The terms I use for to describe them are birth family, growth family, and life family

The first one, birth family, determines your genetics. Take a look in the mirror. What you see is what you got from your birth family. With birth family, you get no choice. You have to play the cards you are dealt.

When there's a *birth family* member absent, like when the father shows up only to contribute to the conception and then is gone, that absence leaves a lot of questions. It leaves a lot of emptiness. It leaves children wondering, *I may look like my dad, but I don't know.* Where do you get that trait from? It might be genetic, it might be environment, but I don't know. Whereas, when you grow up with birth family, you get that frightening realization that you are becoming your parents. You know exactly where all that stuff is coming from. That's birth family. It determines your genetics and you have no choice in that one.

Birth family is defined as our biological family at the moment of our birth. It determines your genetics. You have no choice in the makeup of this family. This is your family of origin. This family constitutes your roots.

We are the product of the contributions of two people: one male and one female. At the moment we are conceived, we have something that can be called birth family. The birth family places emphasis on the two people who brought us into existence. Whenever you talk about family history, you are talking about birth family. When you talk about genetics and predispositions, you are talking about birth family.

Your birth family may continue to be a dominant influence in your socialization and development for your entire life, or your birth family may only exist for a very short time. One or both biological contributors to your existence may be out of the picture shortly after making their initial contributions. Biological parents may be extremely hard to find or extremely hard to get rid of. As we said at the beginning, "Family? It's complicated."

The goal with birth family is to make peace with it.

You can't change it. You have to learn to deal with it. Sometimes, when kids (or adults) are angry (or depressed), they will say something along the lines of, "I didn't ask to be born," or "I didn't get to choose my parents." It's usually an expression of anger, pain, unhappiness, or frustration, but it's ultimately a useless, pointless expression. That's not how it works. Nobody asks to be born. As far as we know, there's not a room full of little pre-born life forms raising their little pre-born hands saying, "Ooh, ooh, pick me, pick me. I want to be born." There was no meeting blotted from your memory at the time of your birth where you logged into your account on ParentMatch.com and swiped left or right on potential pregnancies. And you did not say, "They look nice; send me to there." Nope. That's not how it works.

Two people did things and made choices. And now, through no fault of your own, here you are. Make peace with it. You may have been born to two wonderful people who fell in love and welcomed your birth as the fulfillment of all their hopes and dreams. You may have been born to a single woman who responded to the results of the pregnancy test with profanity. "Oh, ****, I'm pregnant." Your birth may have been wanted, unwanted, planned, unplanned, allowed for, carefully avoided, or feared. You may have been rejected by one person and chosen by someone else, but here you are. Even if you can't make sense of it, at some point, you must accept it and make peace with it. It's part of your history, but it doesn't control your future. It may be where you came from, but it doesn't determine where you are going. It may describe you, but it doesn't define you. You get to do that for yourself.

Does birth family matter? One study found that about 70 percent of adult adoptees express feeling "moderate to significant degrees of uncertainty and ambiguous loss" regarding their birth parents. The remaining 30 percent "expressed security and no apparent [sense of] loss."[3]

The 2018 documentary, *Three Identical Strangers*, examined some of the issues in the nature vs. nurture debate. Three identical triplets were separated at birth. The film compares the influence of their shared genetics versus the influence of their different families and asks the question, "Which was stronger?" In the area of biology and appearance, the genetic influence was obviously dominant. But in areas of identity and socialization, the family they grew up in had the greater influence. This brings us to the second stage of family development.

Growth family is defined as those primary relationships that influence our growth and development.

The goal with growth family is to make sense of it.

This family determines how you develop. You have some influence and choice in this family stage but not very much. As you get older, you gain some influence, but for the most part, other people determine where you live and who you live with. Growth family basically lasts until you're eighteen or whenever you leave and strike out on your own. When you achieve independence, that's kind of the end of the growth family stage.

In the growth family stage, the definition of family becomes more expansive. Siblings and extended family come into play. The genetic influence has been set and now more emphasis is placed on the environmental influences. The growth family is highly significant for developmental reasons. In many ways, it defines who you are and how you think about things. During traditional therapy sessions, it is the answer to the question, "Can you tell me about your family?"

Gaining understanding of your growth family helps you answer the "why" question for yourself. Why do you talk like that? Why do you think that way? Why do you do it that way? On the inpatient unit, I would tell the kids, "If I knew everything about you, your family, how you were raised, and what you've been through, most of your behavior would make perfect sense."

As the growth family ends, you enter a new stage of family development—life family.

Life family is defined as the network of people who support us in life. Unlike the other stages of family development, with life family, you have significant choice.

The goal with life family is to connect with it.

Life family is where you are now. Life family is the people who support you through life, the people you turn to, and the people who are there for you. And with this one, you have quite a bit of part of choice. This family has the most flexibility in it. On the one hand, biological family is family by definition. But very often, biological ties are weakened by time, distance, neglect, or trauma. Relationships can move into the status of "family but not family"

In family, the more continuity, the better. Multiple studies have shown that family stability is a great predictor of academic and other kinds of success. Family stability is a high value that should be pursued at great cost and effort.

When we expand the definition of family to include non-blood (non-genetic) related individuals, what is the criteria for selection when choosing members of your life family? How do you know it's become family? What do you look for when you bestow family status on someone?
In building your supportive Life Family, where do you look for members? What pieces do you already have that you can use? Here ae some places to begin looking.

- *Biological Family.* I am a big fan of biological family becoming life family. This is where you get the maximum benefit of multigenerational relationships.

- *Marriage.* Choosing a life partner is a big deal, and yes, I believe the concept is still valid and beneficial. As of this writing I have been married to my wife for thirty-five years, and my parents have been together for sixty years.

- *Giving Birth and Adoption.* When you create a baby human, you have responsibilities toward your baby. You have become a parent. Adoption is simply becoming a parent without the preceding biological component.

- *Friends.* Some friends are more than friends. When a friendship has significant amounts of all five of the essential traits of family, it should be considered family.

- *Co-Workers.* Is it possible for the people you work with to become like family? Of course. Consider yourself fortunate if you're able to work at a place that fosters these kinds of relationships.

Stop right now and make a list of the people in your life you consider to be family. Review the five essential components of family relationships to help filter the list.

1. Sense of Belonging

2. Unconditional Acceptance

3. Supportive Relationships

4. Shared Experience

5. Time

When you think of these things, who do you think of? Who gives you a sense of belonging? Who do you belong with? Who gives unconditional acceptance? Who do you turn to for support? Who have you shared life with? Who has been a part of your life for a while? These are the people who are functioning as your family.

Now, turn the question around. Who belongs with you? Who do you accept unconditionally, regardless of what they say or do? Who calls you when they need help because they know if you can help, you will? Whose life have you shared? Who have you been with for a long time? These people probably think of you as family.

Here's a blunt, harsh reality moment. Sometimes the reason we don't have a strong, healthy, supportive family is us. That's right, the problem with your family maybe you. Or if you're not the whole problem, you're at least part of the problem. Ouch. That hurts a little bit. But here's how it works. If you're not the problem, then you're not the solution. However, if you're a part of the problem, then you can be part of the solution.

4
HOW DO I TAKE THE FIRST STEP?

Before taking the first step, I have to give some disclaimers. You know, the typical "some exclusions apply, please see store for details" kind of stuff. Maybe I should have put them at the beginning of the book, but here they are. They are essential for directing your expectations for the next chapter and the rest of the book. This is not a "click here to accept the terms and conditions" button. You need to actually read the two disclaimers.

Disclaimer #1: People can change, but you can't change people.

This book is not about giving you the ability to change other people so they can be what you want them to be. It's about giving you the ability to change the *relationship,* so *it* can be what you want it to be. Let me say it again. This book is not about how to change other people so they will become what you want them to be. This book is about how you can change so you can help your family relationships become strong, healthy, and supportive.

Those of you who have a family member who struggles with mental health or addiction issues should know the three Cs of family support. The 2018 movie, *Beautiful Boy,* starring Steve Carrell, shows the tension between supporting someone and trying to change or fix them. As the family sits in a support meeting, you can see a sign on the back wall that says,

I didn't cause it.

I can't control it.

I can't cure it.

The family has to work through the process of learning how to be supportive without being controlling.

I am a big fan of the Serenity Prayer. For those who aren't comfortable with the idea of prayer, I think it's okay to call it the Serenity Statement. In its most common form, it says,

"God, grant me the serenity to accept the things I cannot change, the courage to change the things I can, and the wisdom to know the difference."

Some people know the recovery version of the challenge is—

"God, grant me the serenity to accept the things I cannot change, the courage to change the things I can, and the wisdom to know *that it's me.*"

There is also what I call the advanced version of the statement, which not everybody can understand or accept. But I still think it's true.

"Grant me the serenity to accept the things I cannot change, the courage to change the things I can, and the wisdom to know that I cannot change what I cannot accept. And by accepting it, I begin to change it."

What? Wait. That can't be right.

I didn't believe it at first, either. It was very difficult to accept. But once I stopped putting the two ideas in conflict and started putting them together in harmony, they started producing results beyond what I expected. Let me give you an example.

I have spent a lot of time and effort trying to get my children to change. My attempts were lovingly sincere and well-intentioned, but they were completely ineffective. The more I tried to get them to change, the less accepted they felt and the less influence I had in their lives. When I shifted our relationship away from the change side of the equation and over to the acceptance side, the relationships changed on their own. They got better. In this book, we are going to spend more time changing ourselves than we are trying to get other people to change. As we change, our relationships with others will change. And as the relationships change, our ability to affect change in others will increase, but that doesn't necessarily mean they will change. That brings us to our second disclaimer.

Disclaimer #2: When it comes to families, there are no guaranteed formulas.

Every parent, child, and family is different. Some parents can do everything right and get bad results. Other parents can do everything wrong and have great results.

There was a little girl who was born near Columbus, Ohio. Her daddy was in jail most of her life. Her mom was an addict and not able to take care of her. Children's Services got involved. She bounced around a few foster homes. Finally, her grandparents stepped in and adopted her. One day, they took her to a gymnastics class and found out she was pretty good. The rest is history. This little girl's name is Simone Biles. She won four Olympic gold medals in 2016 and recently won all the gold medals in the US Nationals. She was able to overcome the early obstacles of family and achieve success in gymnastics, but she is still working on the effects of her family issues.

Many people have this misconception that there is a magic formula that produces good kids, and if we can only master the formula, we are sure to be thrilled with how our kids turn out. We want to believe there is a direct line of cause and effect between parent behavior and child behavior. Good parents have good kids, and bad parents have bad kids. If the kids are good, the parents must have done something right, and if the kids are bad, the parents must have done something bad. This is a very old idea, but it's not true. One of my favorite lines from the musical, *Newsies*, is "I'd blame the parents, but he hasn't got 'em."

There's an ancient proverb that says, "The fathers ate sour grapes, and the children's teeth are set on edge." It's recorded in the Bible in Ezekiel 18:2. This proverb appears to reinforce the idea that there is a direct connection between the behavior of the parents and the behavior of the child. If the parents do wrong, then the children will do wrong. The behavior of the children can be explained by the behavior of the parents. But if you read the proverb in context, it says exactly the opposite. The context is "Don't use this proverb anymore; that's not how it works!" The proverb is replaced by the idea that everyone is responsible for their own behavior. Your family of origin does not determine your destiny. Children cannot rest on the goodness of their parents, and they can't use the mistakes of their parents to excuse their own bad behavior.

People with church backgrounds may ask the question, "What about Proverbs 22:6?" That verse says, "Train up a child in the way he should go; even when he is old, he will not depart from it." They exclaim, "There it is. There's the formula. There's the guarantee." They believe that if they do and say the right things at the right time in the right way, then their child will turn out right, and the child has no choice or say in it. That's not how it works. Proverbs are not promises or guarantees; they are general observations about how things usually work.

The proverb gives an early understanding of what modern psychology reinforces, which is the earliest lessons are learned the deepest. The child is the father of the man. There is a Jewish understanding of the proverb that can be paraphrased, "If the child begins in the way of Enoch, he will end in the way of Methuselah." In the Bible, Enoch was a man who walked with

God. He was the father of Methuselah, commonly remembered as the oldest man ever at 969 years, who also walked with God. The faith of the father was carried on by the son. Whatever principles and character traits you want your child to have should be modeled early. And know this: They will retain the values you practice, not necessarily the values you profess.

The problem with looking for a parental formula is that there are some things in life you have a choice about and some things you don't. You don't get to choose your birth family, but you do get to choose how you respond to it.

GENERATIONAL CHOICE

Let's look at the options. And in this paragraph, I'm using the terms *good* and *bad* in a very broad, generic, non-moral sense. *Good* means a healthy and socially functioning person, and *bad* means unhealthy and socially nonfunctioning person. Good is a person who can live well and do good. Bad means one who is not able to live well and do good.
Here are the possible combinations:

- Type 1: Good parents can have good children.

- Type 2: Bad parents can have bad children.

- Type 3: Good parents can have bad children.

- Type 4: Bad parents can have good children.

Types 1 and 2 are easy to understand and easy to accept. The child is exactly like the parent because the apple doesn't fall far from the tree. This seems normal and natural, especially when we are judging the parenting of others. It's Type 3 and 4—when the child ends up nothing like the parent—that we have a hard time understanding or accepting what happened. "How did such wonderful people raise such a rotten kid?" We ask the question but never out loud. Or we wonder, *How did such a wonderful child emerge from such a messed-up home?*.

When I was a youth pastor, one of the girls in the youth group started bringing her boyfriend to church. John was from a terrible home situation. There was no stability in the home and no positive parental role models in his life. Yet from the first time I met him, there was this innate goodness in him. He was smart, kind, sensitive, and intelligent. John would tell horror stories about what was going on in his family, yet somehow, the chaos around him never seemed to disturb the peace within him. He found faith while he was attending our church, and I kept in touch with him through college. John has now grown into an amazing young man and a role model in the community. He was able to evaluate his family heritage and aspire to do better.

I know another family who has three daughters. The eldest daughter embraced her parents' faith and traditions and transitioned from adolescent to adulthood with minimal conflict. The second daughter had significant turmoil in her teenage and young adult years but turned around and found a faith that is in many ways similar to that of her parents. The third sister rejected the faith, traditions, and heritage she was given, but she worked to maintain the relationship with the parents. Same parents, same settings, different outcomes.

Of course, it's an oversimplification to put the parent-child relationships of others into these neat categories. And when we attempt to categorize our relationships with our own children, it becomes more difficult and nuanced. Each of us has the potential of being a good parent and a bad parent. On any given day, we can be either. We can be a combination of good intentions and bad behavior.

The Bible example found in Ezekiel 18 continues. It makes it clear there is *not* a direct connection between the behavior of the parents and the behavior of the child. It emphasizes that each person is responsible for their own behavior regardless of what kind of parents they had. It introduces the idea of generational choice. Each generation has to make a choice and decide what it will do with the heritage it has been given.

The example goes like this. If an individual does good, then he is judged as good based on his own behavior. However, this person may have a child who sees the goodness of the parent, rejects it, and does the opposite of what their parents did. The goodness of the parent does not get passed onto the child because this child takes responsibility for their own behavior. However, this child may also have a child. And this third-generation child may see all the bad things his parents have done and reject them. They may choose to be the opposite of their parents and do good. The badness of the parents does not get passed onto the children. Everyone is responsible for their own behavior.

This helps clarify the responsibility each person has to the generation that came before them and the generation that comes after them. Every generation has the ability to accept or reject its own heritage.

- Each individual should strive to be as good as possible and as good an influence as possible.

- Each individual should identify and embrace the goodness they have inherited from previous generations.

- Each individual should identify and reject the bad they have inherited from previous generations.

Let me share a personal example. My family has a strong history of alcoholism and depression. For the first forty years of my life, I did not drink alcohol at all. Ever. Under any circumstances. The reason for that was that in my early adolescent years, my father told me that we already had enough alcoholics in the family, and we didn't need any more. He told me, "If you start drinking, you may not be able to stop, and it may kill you." And I thought if he caught me, he might.

Children, especially during the teenage years, have what I call a hypersensitive hypocrisy sensor (HHS). They are super sensitive to hypocrisy in their parents, but you already know this is true. If the parent says one thing and does another, the child will pick up on it immediately. This is what causes parents to use that awkward phrase, "Do as I say, not as I do." Parents ... don't say that.

The HHS is not a bad thing. It is what allows younger generations to correct the blind spots of previous generations. Every generation has areas of clarity and every generation has blind spots. Older generations see some things clearly but they are oblivious to other things. The "greatest" generation valued duty, stability, consistency, loyalty, and appearance. But they had blind spots when it came to honesty, transparency, emotional expression, and racism. The boomers came along and addressed the blind spots of their parents. They precipitated a cultural revolution, but they were blind to their own greed and self-indulgence. Now the younger generation is addressing social, economic and environmental issues created by the generation that came before them.

This is how it's supposed to work. Your children will pick up some of your good traits and some of your bad traits. The problem is that you don't get to determine which of your good traits or bad traits they will pick up. That is up to them more than it is up to you.

The key to this whole parenting thing is that you stay involved. Staying involved takes persistence and patience. Persistence = hard work + pain + time. There are some things you are going to have to do as a parent that are very difficult. Parenting is hard work. Or as a friend of mine once put it, "Parenting is a lousy hobby. It's too expensive, and it's often not very much fun." But parenting is not meant to be a hobby. Parenting is a way of life. Do the hard things. Make the hard decisions. Feel the pain of rejection and disappointment your kids will cause you to experience. And keep doing them over and over for a long time. It may take twenty years or so, but those hard decisions will mold your children into individuals who make better decisions throughout their lives.

On the other hand, Patience = time + waiting. Nobody likes to wait. Sometimes with family—parents, children, grandparents, aunts, uncles, cousins—you must wait. There's nothing you can do to get what you want or make good things happen immediately. You must wait for that to happen. What did the father of the Prodigal Son do when his son rejected him and ran away? He waited. It's painful, difficult, and uncomfortable, but sometimes, it's the best response. How do you know how your kids will turn out? You have to wait.

So, if this book is not about getting Mom and Dad to change, and it doesn't have a guaranteed formula for producing good kids, what good is it? What does it have?

- It has some principles you can use to help you deal with the family you have in a strong, healthy, and supportive way.

- It has some guidelines for identifying who in your life functions as family and who doesn't.

- It has some techniques for minimizing family conflict.

- It has some guidance for dealing with the best and worst of family life.

- It is written with the hope that you will be able to appreciate, strengthen, and maintain the good family relationships you have already. And that you will be able to recognize and create new relationships that fill the need you have for a family to belong to.

Remember, everybody deserves a strong, healthy, supportive family.

You can change your family tree in one branch.

Are you ready to get started? Let's go.

To build a strong, healthy, supportive family, you need at least one strong, healthy, supportive person. And that person is you. Remember, when you accept responsibility for your choices, you increase your response-ability.

Nobody likes to find out they're part of the problem. But here's the power and opportunity in it. If you are not part of the problem, you are powerless. You have to deal with it and accept it. But if you are the part of the problem, then you are part of the solution. Now you do have power, and now you can change things and make them better.

The first step in building a strong, healthy, supportive family is to become a strong, healthy, supportive person. Are you willing to accept that goal? Am I saying that to build a strong, healthy, supportive family, you have to work on being a strong, healthy, supportive person? Yes.

Bummer? Yes, I know. But open your mind to it. There are so many stories around you of people who are getting stronger. People around you are getting healthier. How many people have you given support to who are becoming stronger? If you are reading this, it's likely that you are, or at least want to be, a strong, healthy, supportive person. Can you accept that? Can you be that for somebody else?

Once you do that, once you make that commitment, you have to start building relationships with other strong, healthy, supportive people. You know you need to be around other strong, healthy, supportive people. For those of you in recovery, have you already had to let go of some people in your life? You love them, you care about them, but they aren't good for you. They bring out the worst in you. They trip you up. And you had to decide whether you wanted to be strong, healthy, and supportive or not.

This can be tough. Especially if you don't think of yourself as a strong, healthy, supportive person. You may think of yourself as weak, sick, and needy. If you don't think of yourself as strong, healthy, and supportive, you are going to feel uncomfortable around those who are. You will think those people are judging you. You will think those people are better than you, or that they think they're better than you. You will judge yourself as inadequate. You will think, *Those people are getting it done, and I'm failing. Those people all know that I'm just kind of faking it. They're doing well, and I'm just barely holding on. I don't really belong with these people.*

Those negative thoughts will sabotage your recovery. Once you start thinking, *The strong, healthy supportive person is me, and I belong with other strong, healthy, supportive people,* that's where your strong, healthy, supportive family is going to come from.

And the last thing to remember is this. You are not on this journey alone, and your family doesn't expect you to be strong, healthy, and supportive all the time. Give yourself a break and take turns being a strong, healthy, and supportive family member. Let's be honest, nobody can be strong, healthy, and supportive all the time. Nobody. Everybody needs help. That's been said by everybody from the Beatles, ("Help, I need somebody") to Ed Sheeren ("Before I save someone else, I've got to save myself"). The ability to ask for help is necessary for being strong, healthy, and supportive. In a family system, everybody has needs, and everybody has resources. What makes the community strong is when people share their resources to meet the needs of someone else in the community.

That's what it means to be a dynamic family. It's what you've always wanted. It's what the people you love want. It's what the world needs.

PART II

How to Build a Supportive Family

5

PRINCIPLE #1 SHOW UP!
(PRESENCE)

S tarting with the people you already have, the ones you already have a relationship with, the ones who already give and receive acceptance and support, what do you need to do to form this group of people into a strong, healthy, supportive family?

There are four essential skills that are necessary for building a family. If you do these four things, your family will get stronger and healthier, and it will be more supportive. I've made them as simple and memorable as possible.

Show Up!

Listen Up!

Speak Up!

Grow Up!

We're going to go deeper on all of those, but my hope is that when you are trying to figure out what you need to do, you can remember—show up, listen up, speak up, and grow up. That's the pattern that builds healthy families.

PRINCIPLE #1 SHOW UP! (PRESENCE)

If you are going to build a supportive family, you need to be there. Have you heard that the most important step toward winning at anything is showing up? That applies to families as well. When important or traumatic events happen, people take mental pictures of the event. They remember who was there. Have you seen a movie or TV show where the parent promised they would be at an event, and then the child is waiting to see if the parent makes it? It becomes a matter of priorities. Will they say no to the job—or whatever the other thing is—to be there for their kids? When the event starts, and the parent isn't there in the seat, we all feel the pain. It's the issue for Jim Carey's character in *Liar, Liar*. Will he be there for his son? How does the movie, *The Greatest Showman*, end? It ends with P.T. Barnum leaving the show to watch his kids grow up. In the final scene, he is there in the audience, watching his kids perform.

One of the worst moments of my life was my high school senior choral concert. We had an honor solo, but I didn't get that honor. We also had other featured solos as consolation prizes for those of us who had spent our high school years slaving away in the music department. I got one of those solos. My choir director suggested I do the soliloquy from Carousel. It's seven minutes and thirty seconds of baritone solo with a big dramatic high G at the end. I was an eighteen-year-old tenor, and what I remember most about that solo was how badly I splattered that high G all over the auditorium.

I also remember that my parents were there in the audience for that momentous occasion. They were always there. I don't think they ever missed a show, performance, or concert in my life. And they were there for that one. I can still recall in detail us walking out of the high school together. They kept telling me I had done a good job. It wasn't that bad, they said. It was amazing that I had memorized the whole song, and it was all really good. Except for that one note. At the time, I felt like they were lying and trying to be nice. Recently, I listened to an old recording of the performance, and it wasn't as bad as I remembered it. But when it happened, I was mortified. I realize now they were right. I did do a good job. It was amazing that I nailed the whole thing. Except for that one note.

Because we tend to remember who was there. And sometimes, who was not there. The presence of others becomes a part of how we remember the event. That's why it's important to be there. An important part of being family is showing up. Once you decide that being there is important, you have to start making choices and decisions about how to do what is important.

IN ORDER TO SHOW UP, YOU HAVE TO STAY ALIVE.

There's reason I put this point here. If you are struggling with addiction or mental health issues, there is a dangerous thought that might occur to you. The thought is this. *Everyone would be better off if I wasn't here.* That thought can darken to become, *I'll just do everyone a favor and take myself out of the picture.* Have you had that thought? Well, that thought is wrong.

I know this because of a conversation I had with my own father a few years ago. He was talking about his own depression, and he said, "You kids don't know how often I almost didn't come home from work because I thought you would be better off without me." I told him I was glad he chose to come home. Things were rough, and sometimes tense, but we would not have been better off without him. Had he taken his own life, we would never have had that conversation, and I would have suffered a wound that would have never healed.

When you feel like you are the problem, it's easy to think taking yourself out would solve the problem. It won't. If you want to be there for your family, you have to stay alive. One day, death will come for you and take you away from the ones you love. And when it's your time, you have to go. In the end, death doesn't care if you are ready to go or not. That is why we don't invite death to the party. If death wants to come and take you, make it come as an uninvited guest or as a party-crasher. Make death chase you down. When you go, don't go willingly. It's true. Someday we all die. But not like that. Fight for every day of life you can get and then live that day as fully as possible.

This is why the other part of staying alive is taking care of yourself and making healthy choices. It's not enough to just *not* die. If you want to share life with your family, you need to have a life to share. Get some exercise. Make some better food choices. Go get a check-up. Take your medication. If you won't do it for yourself, then do it for those you love.

I'm not fond of making healthy choices, and I don't like taking pills. I also have a family history of high cholesterol. (Remember the impact of birth family?) And I married a nurse. When I was in my forties, I went to the doctor for a checkup, and he discovered my cholesterol was ridiculously high. He said, "You can exercise and diet if you want to, but with your family history and these numbers, you need to be on medication." I went home and talked to my wife. In my own cavalier fashion, I said, "You know, if I'm sitting in the recliner someday, eating pizza, drinking a beer, watching football, and I have a massive heart attack and die, I'm okay with that." She replied, "So am I." She said it in that tone of voice that indicated I should probably pay attention to what she said next. And what she said next was "what I'm not okay with is you having a stroke and me having to spend the last years of my life taking care of you and being angry at you because I know it wouldn't have happened if you would have just taken the medication." My wife doesn't swear much, but I think she may have dropped a non-gratuitous profanity into that sentence. Needless to say, I started taking the medication. Why? For my family. We'll talk more about healthy choices in Chapter 8.

When you are there, be present.

Sometimes, even when we are with family, we aren't really there. When you are with your family, don't just be there, be present. We can be so distracted by other things. It can be work, finances, politics. Social media and screen time can also be big distractions.

Pay attention to your screen time. Screen time is any time you spend looking at a screen. Any screen. TV, computers, smart phones, video games—these all count. A recent report from Market Watch stated that "American adults spend more than eleven hours a day watching, listening to, or simply interacting with media." Let that sink in. If you sleep eight hours a day, that leaves sixteen waking hours. If eleven of them are spent interacting with a screen, that means only four hours are left for interacting with people. Take out driving time, and you may literally be looking at a screen all the time.

There is a practice called phone snubbing or phubbing. It occurs when the information on the screen is more important than the other person in the room. It looks like this: Hold your left hand in front of your face, like you are looking at your phone. Hold up index finger on your right hand in the wait-a-minute gesture. That's phubbing. Don't do that to a family member. Once you become aware of the action, you see it constantly. All I'm saying here is that the best way to find time to be there is to put down the phone, turn off the TV and computer, and pay attention to the people who are with you in real time and space.

When you are there, be sober.

This section is relevant to those who are in recovery. But it's also for those who may depend a little too heavily on some kind of mood-altering substance to deal with family. There's a big difference between drinking at a family event and having to have a drink before going to a family event. My birth family, the family I come from, drank, and some drank heavily. There was no shortage of alcoholics on both sides of the family tree. My growth family, the family I grew up in, did not drink. My father and mother did not drink while they were raising me, and they did not allow us to drink. It doesn't mean it didn't happen, but it certainly wasn't allowed, condoned, or tolerated.

For my part, I chose the straight and narrow. I was a mostly compliant, people-pleasing, middle kid who made the choice to not drink or do drugs. That commitment continued through high school in the 1970s, Christian college and seminary in the 1980s, through the family raising and pastoral years of the 1990s, and 2000s. That commitment didn't change until the kids were raised and I had left church work.

As a musician, I started playing accordion at Celtic Festivals and Oktoberfest, where the main activities are eating, listening to music, and drinking. I remember the first time I had a beer on stage with me at a Celtic Festival. My son was in the audience. I asked him later if it was weird for him to see me onstage with a beer. He said, "I knew you weren't going to finish it." He was right. I didn't. But I accepted his response as a compliment.

Drunk parenting is not good parenting. Buzzed parenting is not good parenting. Even if you are a functioning, harmless, substance abuser, you have to be sober to be a good parent. The question is not "has your family ever seen you intoxicated?" The question is "when was the last time they saw you sober?" Look at the word *intoxicated*. See the word in the middle? It's *toxic*. Being intoxicated is toxic to family relationships.

Some of you may have had to ask yourself, "Is it better to show up buzzed or not show up at all?" Those aren't the only two options. It's better to show up sober. I have a friend who is in recovery. His moment of clarity came when he realized he either had to give up his son or his addiction. That was enough to motivate him to get clean. In the old basketball movie, *Hoosiers*, Dennis Hopper plays the star player's dad, Shooter, who is an alcoholic. He has to get sober to be a part of his son's life. To live sober, you have to have a *why*. "I want to be there," and "I want to be there sober," can be your *why*.

You will have to work to find the time to be there.

I'm going to get to the point and make this easy. Turn off the screen! Time spent staring at TV, video games, smart phones, laptops, and tablets is time that could be spent building your family. Technology is not bad, but it can be a huge time waster. Technology is fine if you control it, but it can be a problem if it controls you. Technology is an excellent servant but a terrible master. Use the technology for it's intended purpose. Complete the task and then turn it off.

You have twenty-four hours a day. And there are four tasks you need to balance during those twenty-four hours. Here are some ways you can use these activities for family building—

- *Eat.* Eat meals together instead of constantly snacking.

- *Sleep.* Identify the routines you can share at bedtime and at the beginning of the day.

- *Work.* Share activities that are productive and do them together.

- *Play.* Plan activities that aren't productive and have fun.

Obviously, you can't be together all the time. But you can look for creative ways to spend time together.

When you can't be there, find a way to be there.

Life happens. You might be away on business, in the hospital, in jail, or in treatment. This is where screens and technology can be useful. You live in the greatest age of technology in human history. Find a way to be there. Find a way to let the people you love know you are thinking about them and love them. Make a way, not an excuse. Notes, cards, messages, calls, gifts—all these things count. The purpose is to let the person know you want to be there.

6

PRINCIPLE #2 LISTEN UP! (COMMUNICATION)

PRINCIPLE #2 LISTEN UP!

"Seek to understand before seeking to be understood."

The second principle is *listen up*. The quote above is not original to me. You can trace it back to Steven Covey's *Seven Habits of Highly Effective People*. He may have gotten it from St. Francis of Assisi. Here's the thing with communication. We all want to be understood. We all want somebody to understand what we're thinking, what we're feeling, and what we're going through. But we don't spend as much time trying to understand the other person. That's why I put this principle as number two.

To communicate effectively, you must understand this:

COMMUNICATION IS A COMBINATION OF TALKING AND LISTENING.

When we have children, we spend the earliest years trying to get them to talk, and then we spend the years after that trying to get them to listen. Here's how this communication process works. When kids are born, they can't talk. They can laugh, cry, and coo. They can jabber. They can communicate, but they don't know any words yet. We can't wait for them to start talking. And then, what happens when they start talking? They won't shut up! They talk. And talk. And talk. And now we want them to *please* stop talking. And then they do. They stop talking. And *all* communication is reduced to sighs, grunts, eye rolls, and requests for rides and money. And all we want is for them to *please* tell us something about their lives, what they're thinking, or how they're doing. And they won't. Isn't that how it usually works?

IF NOBODY IS LISTENING, NOBODY IS COMMUNICATING.

Let's be honest. Most of us are more interested in talking than listening. Most of us spend more time thinking about what we want to say than what the other person is trying to say. Most of us are not very good at listening. This is a problem. Most people are better at talking than listening, but if nobody is listening, then nobody is communicating. Parents, if you're talking and your child isn't listening, all they hear is wah, wah, wah, wah, wah. But you still have to be careful about what you say because when you don't think they're listening, they're listening.

If no one is listening, there is no communication. My wife and I are very different people. Lorrie is a morning person. She shuts down at 10:00 p.m. I am a night person. I usually do my best work starting at 10:00 p.m. In the early years of our marriage when would go to bed together around 10:00 p.m., I was ready to talk. I would share the events of the day and my deepest thoughts and feelings, only to be interrupted by the sound of her deep breathing. (Not snoring—my wife doesn't snore.) She would fall asleep while I was talking. It didn't matter what I had said or how well I had said it; she hadn't heard it. I may have been talking, but I wasn't communicating.

She may have been trying to pay attention, but it wasn't her best time for listening.

To be fair, at other times, she tried to communicate important thoughts and feelings about things at times that weren't good for me. Like, when I'm watching TV. I may have smiled and nodded in agreement while saying, "Okay, dear." But I didn't hear a word she had said. This would cause problems later when I was unable to recall what she had said or what I had agreed to. She offered reminders like "but I told you that yesterday, and you said yes." What I had to learn to do is recognize the tone of voice that indicated, "This is important. You will need to know this later." Whenever I heard that tone of voice, I needed to pay attention and engage good listening skills. Here's what I would do.

- Turn off the TV or mute it.

- Turn to my wife and make eye contact.

- Actively listen to what she's saying.

- Repeat it back to her to make sure I had heard it correctly.

- If it was really important and involved me committing to doing something, I got up an wrote it down so I would remember it.

This probably sounds like a lot of effort, and you're right—it is. Listening is hard work, and it takes effort. But having strong relationships and good communication is worth it.

But what happens when you have done your part, and the other person won't do their part? You've worked hard to listen to them and tried to understand what they are saying, but they aren't meeting you half way? My advice is this.

When the other person stops listening, stop talking.

I had to learn this the hard way with my kids, and I learned it way too late. There were times I wanted to say something to my kids, but I knew they weren't listening. I would keep talking because I wanted to talk. I thought I had something important I wanted to say, and I would take the opportunity to say it because I wanted to be heard and understood. However, when they're not listening, all they heard is that wah-wah-wah-wah-wah-wah-wah sound. Then I'd figure out they hadn't heard what I was trying to say, and that they didn't care. Now I was more angry. Even though they weren't listening, I kept talking. Does that sound familiar?

When it comes to communication, we should pay attention to the law of supply and demand. Are you familiar with what that means? When there is a high supply of something and a low demand for it, when everybody has it and nobody wants it, it has little or no value. On the other hand, if everybody wants it, and there's not very much of it, it has a very high value. Apply that to communication. If you talk, talk, talk, talk, and they don't care, and they're not listening, then what you're saying has very little value. If on the other hand, you wait until you are asked, then they are listening. With the law of supply and demand, the fewer words you say, the more value they have.

There is wisdom in waiting to be asked before sharing your opinion. Have you ever been on the receiving end of someone replying, "Did I ask for your opinion?" I have. The person making the statement usually has a point, and we reply with "I was just trying to help." In that situation, our opinion is obviously not helping.

Free advice is worth what you pay for it. If the supply of words is greater than the demand for the words, the words have little or no value. On the other hand, if the demand for the words is high and the supply is limited, then the words have great value. That is why the Bible suggests that we should "be quick to listen and slow to speak." (James 1:19) And "Let your words be few." (Ecc. 5:2)

Remember that most communication is non-verbal.

Let me give you some examples. What does the sigh with the eye roll and the shoulder shrug mean? If you have teenagers, you know. What do crossed arms accompanied by the words, "Fine. Go ahead. I'm listening," really mean? Since you know most of communication is non-verbal, pay attention to the other person's non-verbals but also pay attention to your own.

In my family, we had this argument about whether I was yelling or not. I didn't think I was yelling, but they all thought I was yelling. I responded with, "I'm not yelling. *THIS IS YELLING!*" What kind of communication is that? After years of doing it wrong, I finally got to the point of realizing that if my wife thinks I'm yelling, and my kids think I'm yelling, I'm yelling. I need to turn down the volume.

How much of communication is non-verbal. Some researchers put the percentage at over 90 percent. The reality is that sometimes the communication is 100% non-verbal. It's called "the look." Parents and teachers have been using it for years. Experienced practitioners of *the look* can say all they need to say without uttering a word.

It's also true that non-verbal communication can be more accurate and reliable than verbal communication. Non-verbals help you realize that sometimes when someone says they're okay, they're really not okay. They also help you identify when kids are lying even before you have proof. The point is … if you are going to listen to understand, you are going to have to pay attention to the non-verbals along with the verbals. Watch posture, gestures, eye contact, rate of speech, volume of speech, and a thousand other nuances to understand the true nature of what is being communicated.

The purpose of communication is to share a thought, feeling, or experience.

Let's do a mental exercise. I'm going to give you a word, and I want you to picture it in your mind. Are you ready? The word is *star*. In your mind, create a picture of the word *star*. Stop reading and do it. It will prove an important point in a few paragraphs.

Got it? Good. Now you can keep reading. When I do this exercise in groups, it works differently because I have them close their eyes. You can't close your eyes and keep reading, can you?

When I ask the group to describe their picture, I get a variety of answers. Some people will describe a shape with five points. It may consist of only lines, or it may be filled in. It's usually yellow or white. Some people will picture a twinkling star in a night sky or a sky filled with stars. Some people will picture a shooting star while others picture a person—someone they think is a star, like Beyoncé or Justin Timberlake. Only occasionally will a person picture the word *star* with the letters S-T-A-R.

Look back at the previous paragraph and read the instructions again. They actually instruct you to picture a word, not an object. Is that what you did, or did you picture a variation of one of the other images? The point is, I have no way of knowing what the word *star* means to you unless you tell me. I have to ask, you have to reply, and I have to listen. Then I have to ask more questions. Communication occurs when the image in my mind matches the image in your mind. Until then, we may think we are communicating, but we may be talking about two very different images.

There are two simple tools you can use to help clarify communication. They are familiar almost to the point of being clichés, but that's because if you use them, they will work.

The first tool is *I* statements. When having an argument or disagreement, develop the habit of using *I* statements. Instead of starting the sentence with the word *you,* you begin with the word *I.* Instead of "you make me angry," you say, "I'm angry." Instead of "you're wrong," you say, "I'm not sure that's right." You want to avoid accusing and judging speech. You want to communicate and share what is going on inside you. You can also say, "I feel like …" or, "It looks (sounds) to me like …"

The other common effective technique is the use of re-statement. It's restating back to the person what they said to make sure you got it right. I use the line, "So, what you're saying is …" If I get it right, then the other person feels listened to, validated, and understood. If I don't get it right, then we start over. Communication occurs when both parties agree on what is being communicated, even if they have different perspectives on it.

Communication is a circle. You talk, and the other person listens. The other person talks, and you listen. And eventually, if you ask enough questions and listen to the answers, you will have the same thing in your mind that they have in their mind. To make sure you're communicating, you can say something like, "We're using the same words, but let's make sure we're sharing the same thought." When you listen enough, ask enough questions, and restate the answers, you can be more certain you are communicating. You can have a conversation like this. "Here's what I'm thinking; is that what you're thinking?" "Yes." "So, what you're saying is …?" "Yes, that's exactly what I'm saying." "So, I understand what you said?" "Yes, you do."

Listening is respect and communication is a gift. When you take the time to understand someone, you show them love. But as we just discovered, good communication is not easy.

RECOGNIZE OBSTACLES TO COMMUNICATION

Communication is complicated. Sometimes it can be difficult. Here are four things that can make communication complicated and difficult.

1. EMOTIONS

It's hard to talk or listen when we are very emotional, and sometimes, emotions can make us say and hear things we never intended. "I was upset" is a common excuse for not communicating or listening well.

When you're communicating and the emotional level goes up, the amount of communication should probably come down. Take a time out. Get yourself back under control. If you keep talking, you might say something you'll regret later. Sometimes you need to retreat to neutral corners and maybe have the conversation at another time.

When you have strong emotions, you go into fight, flight, or freeze mode. When the brain feels attacked, it prepares itself to defend and protect itself. Now, rather than communicating, you are fighting. If somebody says something that hurts you, your natural response is "I'm going to defend myself and try to hurt you back." And that's not good communication. That's probably not what you want to do. Instead, you want to put a buffer in there and take a deep breath. Let the emotions go. Ask yourself, "What do I really want to happen next?" Then ask the other person, "Let me make sure I heard correctly." If you are listening and you ask a question, you can say "Wow, what you said really hurt. What did you mean by that?" And sometimes they will say, "Oh, my gosh, no, I didn't mean that." Other times, they'll say, "You heard me." That's when you know exactly what they intended to communicate.

2. DIFFERENT LIFE EXPERIENCES

As demonstrated in the *star* experience, communication can be difficult between two people who have had very different life experiences. It's hard to picture a black sky filled with twinkling stars if you've grown up in the city. Talking about money can be difficult if one person grew up having it, and the other person grew up never having enough. We tend to interpret the other person's words through our own history and background.

Let's take that idea and apply it to a more complicated concept, like love. Do you freak out when someone uses the L-word? Someone says, "I love you," and you're like ... "*Oh, crap.*" What just happened? The other person just told you they love you, and you wanted to run in the other direction. Your defenses went up, and you backed away. What happened?

Well, let me tell you this story. I grew up in a household where we didn't use that word very often. My mom said, "I love you" every morning, but the only time Dad said it was at the end of this sentence, "I'm doing this because ... I love you." If you grew up with that idea, whenever you hear the word love, you are going to think, *This is not going to be good. I don't want to be around for this. No, thank you, I'm not interested.*

The way we understand words is shaped by our life experiences. When a person says, "I love you," it may be a trigger for you. Or it could be the sentence you want to hear the most.

3. DISTRACTIONS

As mentioned earlier in the story about my wife and I, it's hard to communicate well when there are too many distractions. To have good communication, it's best to minimize distractions so you can focus on listening and understanding what the other is saying and concentrate on finding the best words and tone for what you want to say.

4. FATIGUE

Being tired does not help either our ability to speak or hear. The deeper and more significant the topic of communication is, the more important it is that neither person is overly tired or stressed out. As Vince Lombardi said, "Fatigue makes cowards of us all." We are not at our best we when are tired, and we may lack the courage required to speak and listen well. There is a Biblical admonition against going to bed angry in

Ephesians 4:26, but sometimes, it is wise to get some rest so a heated discussion doesn't become an argument.

If there is no communication, there is no relationship.

It's important to keep the lines of communication open. If you are going to build a family, it's going to take a lot of communication. Nature abhors a vacuum. This is also true when it comes to communication. When there is no communication, the mind tends to fill in the gap. And it usually fills it in with the most negative thoughts possible.

You know how it goes. If you call or text someone and they don't call or text you back immediately, your brain goes into overdrive. Why aren't they responding? Maybe they're dead. Maybe they're mad at me, but why would they be mad at me? Oh, I know why. Really? Why would they be mad about that? They shouldn't be mad about that. But I don't know what else they would be mad about! That's not fair of them. Etc. etc. etc. There are a thousand reasons why the other person may not be responding, and the chances are very slim that you will be able to guess why. But the mind wants to fill in the communication gap with *something*!

If there is no communication, there is no influence.

Communication, the sharing of thoughts and ideas, is essential for having influence. It's hard to be supportive if there's no communication, and it's hard to have influence without communication. Being there is the best gift, and listening is the second-best gift. When you don't know what to say, say nothing. Ask questions instead and listen to their answers. Don't judge.

BUILD COMMUNICATION BRIDGES

Communication can be thought of as a bridge people cross to stay in touch with each other, a way to express thoughts, feelings, and concerns, a path for sharing love. When you think of communication as a bridge, you gain wisdom into establishing and maintaining relationships.

• Don't Burn Bridges

It's an old cliché, but it has an element of truth to it. Relationships have a life cycle. It's natural for them to begin and end, to ebb and flow, to grow stronger and weaker at different times. You burn bridges when you end a relationship in such a way that it's difficult or impossible to repair or re-establish it. It's when you end the relationship by saying or doing something that is almost impossible to forgive. It's when there is so much anger and pain that it becomes unlikely the other person will ever want to communicate with you again.

Sometimes it's good and healthy to end relationships, especially if they are harmful or toxic. But even these relationships should be ended in such a way that the lines of communication are left open. You may not want to communicate with this person again, but you need to allow the possibility that you could if you needed to. Sometimes in life we have to back track and return to people and places we thought we had moved past. In those cases, it's good to leave the bridge standing, even if we think we'll never want or need to cross it again.

But what do you do if you've already burned some bridges?

• Rebuild Old Bridges

Simply because a bridge was burned doesn't mean it can't be rebuilt. Sometimes you can check with the person on the other side and see if there is any interest in rebuilding the bridge. This will probably take some humility and vulnerability on your part. But if you start building on your side, and the other person is willing to start building on their side, old damaged relationships can be rebuilt and restored.

Go slow. Take your time. Try not to get ahead of the other person. The relational bridge may not be as good as new, but it might become passable.

- **Build New Bridges**

Depending on what you have said and done in the past, you may have burned through all your old relationships. In that case, you will need to build new bridges with new people. Sometimes you have to start over. Sometimes you have to create a new family for yourself. Sometimes you have to leave the past behind you. And that includes leaving some people behind. As Steve Harvey once said, "Not everybody that came with you can go with you."

- **Warning: Some Bridges Are Toll Bridges**

Toll bridges are relational bridges you can cross, but you know it is going to cost you to cross them. Like when you visit family members you love, but it's complicated. You want to cross the bridge, but you know it's going to be difficult. You want to visit and communicate, but it takes effort. As long as you're willing to pay the cost, you can cross the bridge.

There were years when my kids were teenagers that it was difficult to keep the communication bridge open. Talking to them almost always cost me something, usually cash. Somehow, they always knew when I carried cash, and then they would talk to me. I learned the response to "hey, Dad" was eventually going to be "how much do you need?"

Sometimes talking with parents can be a toll bridge. You know that if you call or visit, you are going to have to face the awkward questions, accusations, or passive aggressive disapproval of your life choices. But when you compare the cost of reaching out versus the value of maintaining the relationship, you discover it's worth it. When the value is greater than the cost, you can see that it is a positive investment. It is worth paying for the health of your family.

• Warning: Some Bridges Are Troll Bridges

Troll bridges are when you want to communicate and have a relationship with somebody, but there is a gatekeeper that limits access to them. You have to get past the troll to talk with the person you care about.

When this happens, you have to know the secret to getting past the troll. In most literature about trolls, access to the bridge either involves bringing a gift or answering a question. I suggest the same approach to the bridge trolls in your life. Don't ignore them, and you certainly don't want to make them angry. Most of them are honestly only trying to protect somebody they care about, and they may be trying to protect them from you, especially if you have hurt the person they care about in the past.

Try to make friends with the troll. Listen to their questions and learn the answers. Earn their trust. Bring a gift, something that lets them know you respect their position. Eventually, they may let you cross over the bridge.

• Warning: Some Bridges Are Draw Bridges

For various reasons, people may limit access to themselves. Sometimes you can talk to them and sometimes you can't. With a relational draw bridge, you may have to wait. When a person puts themselves behind a draw bridge, they feel safe and protected. Nobody can get in, and nobody can threaten them. But what they discover is that if nobody can get in, then they can't get out.

The key to approaching a person behind a draw bridge is to wait for them to lower the bridge. It must be lowered from the inside, and when the bridge is lowered, you should proceed with caution. People behind draw bridges generally feel frightened and insecure. You don't want to cross the bridge too quickly and make the other person feel like they are being attacked. If that happens, they will raise the bridge again. Sometimes you have to negotiate with the person by yelling over the wall before they agree to lower the bridge and let you in.

7

PRINCIPLE #3 SPEAK UP!
(BOUNDARIES)

Boundaries are the distance at which I can love you and me simultaneously.

—Prentis Hemphill

Once you've done a good job of listening, and you feel like you have a good understanding of the other person and the situation, then the time to speak up has arrived. Speaking up is about setting boundaries; it's about being heard. Some people, maybe most people, talk too much. They try to speak up when they really should shut up.

But there are other people who have trouble speaking up. People with low self-esteem sometimes feel like their thoughts and feelings don't matter. People who are more passive and easy going can make the mistake of being too passive and easy going. They put up with hardships and difficulties until they explode or crash. Some of you are reading this right now and thinking, *That's me. That's exactly what I do.*

When you're the one who always gives in, who always changes their plans for the other person, and always goes with the flow, you can suppress a lot of anger and resentment. That can lead to depression, and depression can be fatal. If you follow that pattern, this is your chapter.

DEVELOP THE ABILITY TO SAY, "NO."

Boundaries are about saying yes and no. They are about determining what is okay and what is not okay, what is acceptable and is not acceptable in a relationship. All relationships have boundaries. In fact, relationships are defined by their boundaries. If you look at relationships like government/citizen, employer/employee, husband/wife, parent/child, teacher/student, you can see that all relationships have boundaries. All relationships have rules and expectations. All relationships have areas of behavior that are not appropriate or okay. In a healthy relationship, both sides work together to agree on mutually acceptable boundaries. In a healthy relationship, both parties have the right to say no.

Since this is a book on families, somebody may be asking, "Are you saying that children have the right to say no to their parents?" Of course, I am. I am a strong advocate of parental authority and respect for parents. I believe that "Honor your Father and Mother" is a life-long mandate, but no child should feel powerless in a relationship. Obviously, if a parent asks a child to do something harmful, hurtful, abusive, illegal, or inappropriate, the child should feel like they have the ability to say no and to refuse. There may be negative consequences, discipline, or punishment that the child may wish to avoid, but they should never feel like they have no choice in the matter.

SAY "NO" TO LESSER THINGS SO YOU CAN SAY "YES" TO BETTER THINGS.

It's important in relationships to keep the concepts of yes and no together. In my early years as a parent, I was definitely out of balance on the negative or no side of the equation. I had to learn the principle, "Say yes whenever you can, so that when you say no, it sticks." There's a sign on my dad's wall that says, "You can have everything, but you can't have it all at once." Another one says, "You can do anything, but you can't do everything." Life is full of choices. Some would say your life is defined by the choices you make.

Boundaries are never only about saying no. In recovery, if the only goal is not to use, that's a negative goal. And guess what you're thinking about all the time? Not using. So, what are you thinking about? Using. So, what's going to happen? Unless you have a better thing to do and a better thing to think about, you're going to relapse. Once you get to the point of saying, I'm saying no to a bad thing because I want to say yes to a good thing, you will gain strength in your decisions and start making real progress in your life.

DEVELOPING PERSONAL BOUNDARIES

The most important person to be able to say "no" to is yourself.
The first control is self-control. If you cannot control yourself, you will feel out of control. If you always feel out of control or if you're always losing control, you will lose self-respect and injure your relationships with people who care about you. If you cannot control yourself, you will be controlled by others.

It's a personal victory to be able to maintain some level of control and say, "That's not going to happen." When you violate a personal boundary, your self-respect goes down. You hate yourself. You give up. You lose hope. Maintaining a personal behavioral boundary means you are able to say, "I don't do that." It means being very strict and honest with yourself.

Respect your own moral boundaries.

Everybody has a sense of right and wrong. It's called a conscience. When you do things that are within your moral boundaries or are supported by your morals, you feel good about yourself. You feel like you did the right thing. When you violate your own moral boundaries, you feel bad about yourself. You feel guilty, and you lose self-respect.

When it comes to your conscience and sense of morals, you can change your boundaries, but you can't compromise the ones you have. For instance, if you are raised in a religious system that forbids eating pork, you may grow up with a moral boundary that says "no" to eating pork. But imagine that one day, probably in your teens, you are driving down the street with a friend and you smell something delicious. "What is that marvelous smell?" you ask your friend. They reply, "That is the smell of a bacon cheeseburger." "I must have one," you exclaim, and you drive into the parking lot of a fast food burger joint. Standing inside, you experience a moral dilemma. You have been taught that God forbids eating bacon, but it looks and smells so good. So, you give in to temptation and take a big juicy bite of your bacon cheeseburger.

Instantly, you fall in love with bacon. "Where have you been all my life?" you ask. Now you have a problem. Your behavior is outside your moral boundaries. You can do one of two things: you can change your behavior, or you can change your boundaries. You can change your behavior and say, "That was delicious, but I want to obey God's rules, so I will never eat bacon again." Or you can change your boundaries and say, "That rule is ridiculous. There's nothing wrong with eating bacon. I'm going to eat it and enjoy it."

What you can't do is continue without resolving the moral conflict. If you continue eating bacon while feeling it's wrong to do so, you will feel guilty. If you don't resolve the guilt issue, you may start lying about eating bacon, hiding bacon so no one knows you eat it, and obsessing about the next time you can sneak away to have some bacon. Now, you're addicted to bacon.

You already have a set of morals and values when it comes to what is appropriate in family relationships. They show up in the expectations you have of fathers, mothers, grandparents, and children. You have a sense of how things ought to be and how they should be. When your behavior matches your sense of ought-ness and should-ness, you will feel good about yourself and your behavior. When there is conflict, you will feel bad about yourself and lose self-respect.

It is not the purpose of this book to give you a set of moral boundaries. The purpose here is to help you recognize the set you already have and develop the self-control to live within them. And remember, your conscience is not infallible. Some of the rigid moral boundaries you have developed may need to become more fluid. Other moral boundaries may become more rigid with age. I know that moral growth and development has been an important part of my own experience. There are behavioral prohibitions I used to hold I now think are okay. Developing your moral core over time is called wisdom.

Respect your own behavioral boundaries.

Behavioral self-control is the ability to get yourself to do the things important to you and keep yourself from doing things that make you feel bad about yourself. When you have enough self -control to do what you know is right, your self-respect goes up. When you lose self-control and do something you think is wrong, your self-respect goes down.

It is also important to have relational boundaries.

If we are going to have strong, healthy, family relationships, we have to set boundaries with others. Why do people treat us the way they do? Because we let them. Or as Dr. Phil puts it, "We teach people how to treat us." Setting boundaries isn't about trying to control or change people, it's about maintaining the relationship and making it stronger. We don't set boundaries on relationships we don't care about, we abandon them.

The key to maintaining good boundaries in relationships is to understand that in any relationship, *you only control half of the relationship.* You are responsible for your thoughts, feelings, and behavior, and the other person is responsible for their thoughts, feelings, and behavior. You are not responsible for theirs, and they are not responsible for yours.

That doesn't mean these areas aren't connected. If I do something that hurts or angers a family member, I am responsible for what I did. And if it was not my intention to hurt or anger them, I should take responsibility for my behavior, apologize, and ask for forgiveness. We can help with the process of restoring and healing the relationship, but we can't blame our behavior on others or accept responsibility for the behavior of others.

Manipulation is bad for relationships; we manipulate someone when we try to control both halves of the relationship. Sometimes guilt and fear are used to make one party do something they are not okay with. It violates their personal moral boundaries or values. Manipulation will eventually suck the life and health out of a relationship. As we said before, in a healthy relationship, both parties have the freedom to say no to various aspects of the relationship, including being in the relationship itself. Both parties are free to discontinue the relationship if it becomes harmful or toxic.

You can't control or change other people in a healthy relationship. If you're trying to control both halves of the relationship, or if you are trying to change the other person so they can be what you want them to be, then the relationship is becoming toxic. The same is true if someone is trying to control or change you into being what they want you to be. Relationships centered on power and control are not healthy.

They can be healed but only if both parties are willing to address the toxicity.

Keep your self-respect

Healthy relationships, especially healthy family relationships, are built on mutual respect. A healthy self-respect is critical for being in any healthy relationship. If we don't have a healthy level of self-respect, we will say and do things to injure the relationship. We may even sabotage an otherwise healthy relationship because we don't feel worthy of being in it.

Family relationships may be able to survive the loss of respect, but it is difficult to maintain healthy family relationships once respect has been lost. We may still love, support, and care for them, but it will be difficult to do so when they have lost our respect. Even though unconditional acceptance and supportive relationships are essential to creating the feel of family, these qualities operate separately from the level of respect received or given. It is possible to say, "I still accept you as part of the family, and I support you as a person, but I have completely lost respect for you at this moment."

Avoid the Disrespect Trap

There is a common misconception about how respect works. The misconception goes like this: "If you respect me, then I'll respect you. If you disrespect me, I'll disrespect you back." There are several problems with this approach to respect. The first is that if you take this approach, you have given away all your power. You have given control of both halves of the relationship to the other person. They are setting the tone of the relationship, not you. They are controlling the quality of the relationship, not you. They are taking the proactive role while you are in the reactive role.

The second problem is that if you have a low level of self-respect (if you don't respect yourself very much), you will have a predisposition to see, hear, and feel disrespect from others, whether it is there or not. Why should the other person respect you if you don't respect yourself? You will tend to interpret the other persons behavior as disrespect whether they mean it that way or not. You will assume others are giving you the same disrespect you give yourself.

There is a way to break out of that trap and disrupt the cycle. You have to give the respect to others you want to receive. You give others respect, not because of who they are, but because of who you are. You treat others with respect to maintain your own self-respect. Does that mean you will give respect to some people who don't deserve it or haven't earned it? Yes—and doing that will take some humility and self-control on your part. But it's worth it. Again, we want to be able to give respect, even when the other person behaves in ways we do not respect.

One good way to maintain healthy relationships is to pay close attention to pronouns. I learned to do this when my wife would say, "You know what I think *we* should do?" That pronoun *we* could have one of several meanings. It could mean, "Here's what I think *I* should do," or "Here's what I think *you* should do," or "Here's something I think *we* should do together." I learned to respond by asking, "How are we using the word *we* in this sentence?" In healthy relationships, it's helpful to think in these terms.

I do me. You do you. We do us.

I still exist as an individual person. You still exist as an individual. But there is this new shared identity called *us*. Think of it in terms of two overlapping circles.

You don't want to lose your own identity in the *us* of a relationship. This can happen in long term relationships. You don't want the relationship to become 100% us, where I lose me, and you lose you. The us section needs to be the place where the me and the you come together and overlap. The more overlap there is, the stronger the relationship, but you don't lose yourself in trying to become what the other person wants you to be. In a healthy relationship, you become more fully you as you interact with the other person being fully them.

A Warning about Changing Boundaries

Whenever there are disputed boundaries in a relationship, you can expect friction. And when you try to change the boundaries in an existing relationship, you can also expect conflict. You can expect the other person to get angry. Why? Because they already had a set of rules and boundaries, and they thought you agreed to them. The old boundaries were working for them. When you try to reset the boundaries, insist on mutual respect, and take control of your half of the relationship, the other party will often feel attacked. They will either be open to renegotiating the boundaries, or they won't. If they are open to negotiating new boundaries, then you have to decide whether the current boundaries are acceptable to you. If that happens, then keep the relationship. If they are not open to negotiating new rules and boundaries, then you may have to make significant changes to your half of the relationship.

8

PRINCIPLE #4 GROW UP! (PERSONAL GROWTH)

Grow up! That sounds a little harsh, doesn't it? Nobody likes to be told they need to grow up. I've seen memes that say things like, "If you haven't grown up by age forty, you don't have to." Or, "Growing old is mandatory; growing up is not." However, there comes a time in life when we all need to grow up. Growing up is when you become an adult and start putting away childish things. It's an idea that is found in the Bible. It says, "When I was a child, I behaved like a child, I thought like a child, I acted like a child. When I grew up, I had to put away the childish things." (I Corinthians 13:11)

There is a set of behaviors I call two-year-old coping skills. Typical two-year-old coping skills include whining, pouting, stubbornness, and temper tantrums. When we see that behavior, we say, "You're acting like a two-year-old." Which is perfectly acceptable if, in fact, you are a two-year-old. But the longer you use two-year-old coping skills, the more inappropriate, sad, and pathetic they become. Have you seen an adult resorting to two-year-old coping skills, and you wanted to say, "Really? We're pouting and whining and throwing temper tantrums? That's what we're going with on this one?"

When you say it that way, it sounds bad. But yes, that's often what is happening.

This is the point where the book on building a family becomes a book on self-improvement. We all want to have a strong, healthy, supportive family, but we usually are thinking of ways our family can be more supportive to us. Here is where we begin to focus on how you can be more supportive to them. If you want to be a part of a strong, healthy, supportive family, you have to work on becoming a strong, healthy, supportive person.

Let's connect some dots from Chapter 2, "Why Families Are Necessary." Remember, we said there are three primary goals of any family. They are safety/survival, personal development, and social development. These three primary goals correspond to the three-word description of the family we want to build. We want it to be strong, healthy, and supportive. Strength is related to our ability to survive. Healthy has to do with our personal development, and supportive has to do with our social development.

What is strength? Strength has to do with power and flexibility. Strength is the ability to withstand pressure. Some people call it resilience. As Rocky Balboa said, "It's not about how many times you get knocked down, it's about how many times you can get back up." Strength has to do with exertion and endurance. It's the ability to do work. Strength can be defined as "the ability to move and not be moved." Wikipedia gives the definition as, "The ability to withstand an applied stress without failure." These definitions are borrowed from the world of physics, but they can also be applied personally.

Do you consider yourself to be a strong person? If not, why not? Do you feel weak? There's an interesting relationship between strength and weakness. For those of you who exercise regularly, how do you feel after an intense workout? At the end of a good workout, you feel weak. Sometimes you do reps to the point of failure, which means you keep going until you absolutely can't do one more repetition. You feel weak, and you have failed at the last thing you tried to do. Then your muscles ache. What is happening in the middle of feeling weak, going to you can't go any more, and all the pain? You are getting stronger. That's why they say, "No pain, no gain."

The Bible teaches the principle that power is perfected in weakness and presents the paradox that "when I am weak, that's when I'm strong." (II Corinthians 12:10) The key to finding our strength is in accepting our weakness. Knowing when we are weak helps us become strong.

What is health? Health has to do with harmony and balance. Systems that work together are said to be healthy. Plants, animals, social structures, and eco-systems that are in harmony and in balance are said to be healthy. When the physical systems in my body are working together and in balance, I am healthy. When the systems are injured, diseased, or in stress, I am unhealthy.

There are four areas in which you want to be healthy: mental, emotional, physical, and spiritual. My wife is a nurse and works primarily in the area of physical health. For twenty-five years, I was a pastor and helped people maintain spiritual health. Now I work in the area of mental health. Guess what? They are all connected. If you lose your physical health, it will affect your mental and emotional health. When was the last time you had the flu? It was primarily a physical health issue. But how did that affect your emotions? Were you happy or sad? How did it affect you mentally? Did you feel like tackling some tough mental challenges? How about spiritually? Did you pray? All these systems are connected.

Which of your four systems do you feel is the healthiest right now? Which one is the least healthy? What can you do to improve your health in each of the four areas? If you are going to build a strong, healthy, supportive family, you are going to have to take care of your health.

What does it mean to be supportive? Being supportive simply means contributing to the success of someone else. A supportive family is one that celebrates the accomplishments and successes of each member.

I am convinced the best part of life is this.

"Having something to do and someone to do it with. Having something to share and someone to share it with."

I don't know that life gets better than that. To be supportive, you must have something to share and someone to share it with. It may be strength, wisdom, experience, money, or time. It can be anything, but you must have enough of it to share, and you must have someone to share it with.

Think of the people you consider to be family. What can you do to support them? What do they need that you have to give? We don't work on self-improvement and personal growth only for our own benefit. We work on improving ourselves so we can be supportive of the people we care about.

In a healthy family or community system, everyone has needs, and everyone has resources. There are things we have to give and things we need to receive. We offer what we have to give, and we allow ourselves to receive what others have to offer. The goal is not independence. We don't want to be perpetual toddlers saying, "I'll do it myself," or an angsty adolescent saying, "I don't need anybody." We want to need others, and we want to be needed. But the goal is not to be codependent. It's not good to lose ourselves in giving to others or define ourselves only by what we have to give. We shouldn't need to be needed. That's out of balance and therefore, unhealthy. The goal is to be interdependent. Sometimes I help you; sometimes you help me. I offer to the family what I have to give, and I am willing to accept the help and support that others have to give.

This requires the best kind of humility. Humility has been described this way. "It's not thinking less of yourself; it's thinking of yourself less." It's knowing who you are, who you are not, where you are strong, and where you are weak. It's knowing where you fit and also where you don't. Humility is a virtue you must have to be strong, healthy, and supportive.

Let's focus on four areas of life in which we can set growth goals.

1. MENTAL GROWTH—LEARN SOMETHING NEW

If I asked you what's something new that you've learned in the last month, could you give me an answer? Are you staying sharp? Are you learning new things? Are you staying open to new ideas? It is easier to learn new things now than ever before in human history. Do you have a smart phone? Take it out and Google something. Anything. All the accumulated knowledge of humanity is at your fingertips. Take advantage of it.

For those in recovery, recovery is all about learning to think differently. Let's take a moment and clarify two terms—brain and mind. Your brain is what you think with. Your mind is how you think. In computer terms, your brain is the hardware, your mind is the software. Your brain is the processor, your mind is the program, the operating system. In making progress in recovery, you need to update your operating system. You have to change your programming. You have to renew your mind and develop new ways of thinking. There has to be a difference in how you used to think and how you think now—that's what mental growth is.

2. EMOTIONAL GROWTH—WORK ON BECOMING EMOTIONALLY STRONGER

Emotional growth is about getting emotionally stronger and gaining resilience. Emotional growth is about learning to accept your feelings. And here's what this looks like. There are days when you say, "If one more bad thing happens, I am not going to be okay." And that's being emotionally weak. Emotional strength says, "I've been hurt, disappointed, and rejected. I've gotten bad news, but I'm okay. I can handle it.

I'll get through it. I'm fine." We don't deny emotions, and we don't try to control emotions, but we do acknowledge and accept them.

One of the hardest things about living sober is learning to deal with emotional pain, knowing that you know how to make the pain go away. You don't want to feel this, but you can't make it go away. It is part of your life, so you have to feel it and get through it. Emotional growth is being able to say, "This is what I'm feeling, it's emotional, it's terrible, but it will pass, and I can handle it."

3. PHYSICAL GROWTH—DO MORE. EAT BETTER. REST.

Physical growth is the simple stuff. Exercise. Eat right. Get enough rest. You have a body, and you have to live in it. If it feels bad, you feel bad. If you eat like crap, you feel like crap. I didn't design the system; I can only describe how it works. You must make some changes in how you manage the system if you want to grow. You need to exercise. Right now, if you stood up and ran in place for ten seconds and then sat down, you would feel better. You'd be more awake and alert. Your emotions would adjust, and you would feel like you can do more. Exercise is as effective as anti-depressants for treating mild to moderate depression. Do something, get out, get moving, and get enough rest. If you are not sleeping at all, get some help with that.

You must take care of yourself physically. I know, eventually time takes its toll, and death takes us all. But in the meantime, optimize your health to optimize your life. I am by no means an expert of physical health, but I do have a few simple principles I try to follow. These constitute the framework for my physical growth goals.

Do more. Eat better. Rest.

That's it. It's not very complicated, but it will lead you in the right direction.

4. Spiritual Growth—Connect with Your Meaning and Purpose

You have to connect with something bigger than yourself, something other than yourself, for life to have meaning and purpose. This is not about religion. This is about knowing who you are, why you're here, and what you're doing with your life. At some point, your growth becomes spiritual. You must find that place and activity that lets you feel, *This is what I want to do. This is who I am. This is what I was made for.*

I believe we are spiritual beings. The spirit is what gives life meaning and purpose, and we can't live life without meaning and purpose. I'm so glad that in the Marvel Universe the Infinity Gauntlet includes a soul stone. (Some of the Marvel movie geeks will understand that reference.)

Spiritual growth is when we connect with something bigger than ourselves, something other than ourselves. The soul is the part of us who wants to know who we are, where we fit, and why we're here.

Your Four Life Batteries

Here's what I want you to do right now. Think of yourself as containing four rechargeable life batteries. These four batteries are Mental, Emotional, Physical and Spiritual. If you drain all four of your batteries until they are empty, you will turn off, and you will lose the ability to function. You must find the things in life that help you recharge your batteries.

Give yourself a power level for each of your life batteries. 100% is fully charged, 2% is about ready to turn off. Which batteries are fully charged? Which batteries are almost fully drained? What can you do to recharge your batteries? If reading this book is recharging your mental and emotional batteries, then keep on going into the next section. If reading this book is draining your batteries, put it down and go do something fun. Seriously. Do it.

PART III

HOW TO HANDLE FAMILY FRICTION

9

UNDERSTANDING FAMILY FRICTION

If we're going to look at this concept of how to build a family, we're going to need to talk about the existence of family friction. You've probably not heard of the concept of family friction. It's a different way of looking at the tension that occurs in family relationships. If I had put the term *family conflict* in the title, you would probably have a better idea of what I'm talking about. But I want to try to change the way you look at family conflict so you start thinking about how to manage family friction.

Many family relationships are like an extended game of bloody knuckles. Have you ever heard of that game? It's where two people face each other with their fists extended. One person tries to hit the other person's knuckles before they can react and withdraw. If you succeed in hitting the other person, you get to keep going. If you fail, then the other person gets to try to hit your knuckles. The game is basically two people trying to hurt each other without getting hurt themselves. Whoever hurts the other person more than they get hurt wins. If the goal is to see if I can hurt you more than you hurt me, that's conflict. That's reducing the relationship down to winners and losers and hurt and pain. It's only two people continually hitting and hurting each other. Some people's family relationships are an extended game of bloody knuckles.

If you are stuck in one of these relationships, but it's a family relationship you want to hold onto, how do you stop hitting and hurting each other? Here's what most people try to do first. They think, *Maybe if I hit the other person hard enough, they'll stop hitting me back.* But what usually happens is that both people are thinking that. And both people keep hitting each other harder, and nobody stops because they are both trying to win, and they are both waiting for the other person to stop.

One of the things you can do differently is to go into a negotiation mode. Let me give you an example. One day on the inpatient unit, a kid took a swing at me. He swung at me with his right hand, and I caught his fist mid-air with my left hand. Needless to say, he was a bit startled and unsure about what to do next. If you take a swing at somebody and they catch your punch, you probably shouldn't throw another one. Here's what catching the punch says. It says, "I'm not trying to hurt you, but I'm not going to let you hurt me, either." That's an intervention. Catching the punch says, "We're not going to do this anymore. Let's stop this right now." But you can't stand there holding the punch forever. At some point, you have to let go. And very often, when you let go, the other person starts punching again. When we let go and the person starts punching again, our tendency is to go back to the bloody knuckles game.

Part of dealing with conflict as friction is staying open to it. When you practice boxing, one person holds up an open hand to allow the other person to hit it. Keeping an open hand helps to absorb the blows, and it doesn't hurt as much. You can handle a little bit of conflict. We've disrupted the bloody knuckle game a little bit. If you can get the other person to open up their hand, then when they come together, it's clapping. You end up getting applause, and you can join hands, interlock fingers, and form a strong bond.

But sometimes, that doesn't work. The other person doesn't open up, and you have to walk away. There's only so much hitting you can tolerate. Eventually, the open hand starts waving good-bye, and you have to take yourself out of the way. When you do, the other person may continue their hitting motion. They are used to it, and it works for them. But they soon discover it's a meaningless and awkward motion. It's not much fun, and it's not very rewarding when there's nobody there to hit.

Then one of two things will happen. They will either find somebody else to play bloody knuckles with, or they will open up and give the "please come back" motion.

If that is family conflict, what is family friction? Why are we using the term friction? Friction is simply rubbing the two hands together; it doesn't necessarily mean conflict. Two hands rubbing together is the sign of somebody getting warmed up to do something. Friction is not necessarily bad. *Friction is only resistance.*

Let's use planning an event as an example. You know what you want to do, and you suggest it, but you meet resistance. "No, I don't think that's what I want to do." "Well, how about if we do this?" "No, that doesn't sound good either." It's not conflict, but it's *resistance.* It might be a discussion. It might be an argument. You might not be on the same page. It's only friction. Once you realize it's only friction, you can respond to it differently.

What is the source of friction? It's simple: *Friction is just two people, in contact, in motion.* That's all it is. Any two people in contact and in motion are going to experience some friction. They can love each other. They can care about each other. They can want to help each other. They can be supportive of each other. But when you have two people in contact and in motion, there's going to be friction.

Think about house guests as an example. You invite them to come stay with you because you love them. But as they say, "House guests and fish start to stink after three days." Even though everybody involved is a good person and everybody has the best of intentions, you have two or more people in contact and in motion, so there's going to be friction.

The difference between friction and conflict is that *conflict puts people in opposition.* Let's be honest. Some people like conflict. Right? And that's okay. That's not bad. There's a lot of conflict in the world, and some people are better at dealing with it than others.

I personally don't like conflict. Both my wife and I are conflict avoiders. About five years into the marriage, we had to learn how to do conflict. Things were starting to build up, and we were both avoiding them. We had to learn to be more direct, more blunt, and more honest. When we started to make the change, it freaked the kids out. They were initially threatened by it and thought that since we were starting to argue more, that we were going to separate. We had to explain to them that we were getting better, and that the relationship was actually growing and developing.

If you like conflict, you have to learn to pick your battles. There is a lot of conflict out there, and some of it's worth fighting for. Some of it is not. We need people who are okay with conflict to get into our wars and battles and fight for us. Some people like that kind of thing, and they respond to it by saying, "Sign me up. I'm at home. I am good at it. Show me where the conflict is, and I'll run toward it. Did you think I was going to back down, change my mind, and let you walk all over me? No, that's not really what I do." There's nothing wrong with that. Some people like conflict, and some people hate it. Some people avoid conflict, and some people create it.

Do you know any people who bring conflict and drama with them? Have you ever asked yourself, *Why? Why is there always drama and conflict when this person is around?* It's because they like it, and they are comfortable with it, and they're good at it. If you like something, you're comfortable with it, and if you're good at it, you are going to keep creating it.

On the inpatient unit I used to work on, some of the patients grew up in homes marked by constant conflict. They hated it, but they felt comfortable with it. We ran a respect-based unit, and the rule was "I'll respect you, you respect me, and we want you to respect yourself and each other." It freaked them out. They didn't know how to handle it or respond to it, so they would respond by recreating the conflict and chaos they were comfortable with at home. And some of them were very good at it. They would sit there and think about what they could do to make somebody angry. They would sit and watch me and try to figure out my weak points and try to make me angry. Then, if I got upset and started yelling at them, they felt right at home. Once everybody was angry, yelling at each other, and hating themselves and everybody else, they felt comfortable and in familiar surroundings. They knew how to handle that situation.

It was very difficult to get them to understand they didn't need to do that. It was okay for us to have friction. We had fifteen kids on a unit, trying to get them to the same place at the same time. There was going to be some friction, but we didn't have to create conflict.

Once we view something as conflict, *it limits our perspective.* It becomes a win or lose situation. I have to win, and you have to lose. Or it becomes a situation of right and wrong. One person feels like they are right, and they have to let everybody else know they are right. Have you ever heard the phrase, "living all alone in Rightville?" That's when the person realizes that even though they were right, nobody is talking to them. Everybody has left them, and they have no friends. But at least they were right.

Maybe if the situation had been handled as friction, it wouldn't have needed to become conflict. Sometimes we want the other person to know and understand we were right. But the truth is that may never happen. And there's the possibility you may not have been right after all. In those cases, it's better to know how to manage friction better.

Strong wills can become opposing forces. But they don't need to be. If you are in a relationship with a strong-willed person, good for you, especially if you are also a strong-willed person. When you get two strong-willed people moving in the same direction, you can get some stuff done. They can be a power couple. When the kids are looking at unified, strong-willed parents, they know they're done. They might as well give up and do what they're told. But you want those strong wills moving in the same direction. Otherwise, it can become a problem. I remember seeing an old picture of a wagon, and it had two strong horses hooked up to it, one on each end of the wagon, pulling in opposite directions. The cart didn't move, and the horses grew more tired. You either have to put both horses on the same end of the wagon pulling in the same direction, or you have to unhook one of the horses. Otherwise, you're not going to get anywhere.

Unlike conflict, *friction keeps people working together.* Friction can happen if you are moving in opposite directions, but it can also happen if you are moving in the same direction at different speeds. Let me give you an example from my own house. We had a son who was living with us, and it was time for him to move out. We all agreed on that, were all moving in the same direction, and wanted the same thing. He wanted to move out. My wife wanted that. I wanted that. But we were all moving at different speeds. Even though we agreed on the outcome, there was a lot of friction. Should we do something now or later? Maybe this is the right response, but the wrong time. Maybe we should wait. Maybe we should act. Maybe we should say something. Maybe we shouldn't say anything. What did we do? We watched his responses and had a lot of discussions. We experienced a lot of friction, but we managed to get to the destination, and we achieved the goal.

Friction isn't bad or good; it exists as part of life. Friction can be managed to keep the relationship healthy and functioning. Just because you have friction in the relationship doesn't mean it's not working. It may mean that it is working. Sometimes you have better arguments than you used to have because you are finally strong and honest enough. That's progress.

One positive benefit of friction is that friction can provide traction, and traction is necessary for progress. If you are stuck in the snow or mud and your tires are spinning, you need more friction. You need traction. If you feel like you are in a relationship and you are only spinning your wheels and not getting anywhere, you may need to introduce some friction to gain some traction. Somebody may need to offer some resistance. Sometimes one person offering resistance is enough to help the other person gain traction. When it comes to your car brakes, you want to have friction. If there's no friction, there's nothing to slow you down.

Shaping is another positive benefit of friction. If you work with wood, you know the value of sandpaper. Sandpaper is only applied friction. That's the force that smooths out the rough edges. Is that a pleasant process? No. But if you are a good person and you are in a relationship with a good person, you want to help shape them, and help them become the best version of themselves. You want to have the effect of smoothing out the person's rough edges.

If you had met me thirty-five years ago, you would not have liked me very much. Not even my wife liked me back then. And I didn't like myself very much, either. Her first impression of me was that I was arrogant. I was really just very insecure. We had a mutual friend try to hook us up, and my wife's thought was, *No, thanks.* The shape that I am in now is a result of a lot of sanding and shaping by a very strong-willed person. She saw the potential in me, but she was not going to put up with my stuff. There's been some friction, but it has helped to shape me into a better person, and that's been good for me.

10

ACCEPTING FAMILY FRICTION

Friction is only resistance. It's a result of two objects, in contact, in motion—or in this case, two people, in contact, in motion. When you know this, you can move toward accepting it. Much of the stress and anxiety in life is a result of our struggling to accept things we can't change. Friction will be a part of every relationship in life. Accept it.

There are some steps we can take to help us accept the friction that is a normal part of even healthy relationships. I want to lay out for you a simple system. It's simple, but it's not easy. It's easy to memorize, but it's not easy to implement. Here's what I want you to memorize.

Look—Listen—Love—Let Go.

That's the system. You can commit it to memory. You can integrate it into your response process, and it can become a reflex. Look at it again and say it out loud.

Look—Listen—Love—Let Go.

If I'm going to respond appropriately to a situation, I have to be able to accept it for what it is. I have to respond to what is actually happening, not to what I think is happening.

When you are dealing with family and there's a crisis, argument, or unpleasant emotional explosion, this approach will lead you to a good response if you give it a chance. We're going to unpack it and explain it. But there's something you have to learn to do first.

TAKE A DEEP BREATH.

Seriously. Go ahead. Right now. While you are reading this book. Take a deep breath. Inhale slowly and let your lungs fill up with air. Now exhale slowly and feel the air leaving your lungs. Do it. You feel better, don't you? Go ahead and do it again.

This is what I call *Coping Skill #1*. When you feel angry, threatened, or frustrated, take a deep breath first. Because when you feel like that, the rational part of your brain shuts off, and you go into fight, flight, or freeze mode. You are not thinking, you are reacting. Fight, flight, or freeze are usually not the best responses for dealing with family friction.

You probably have a preference for one of those responses. Which is it? In conflict, when you feel angry, threatened, or frustrated, which one do you do? Do you fight? Do you run away (flight)? Or do you shut down and do nothing (freeze)? Teach yourself to take that deep breath first. This allows you to re-engage the rational part of your brain. Now you can come up with a better response.

I call that better response the family friction response process. (The *FFRP*. Mental health professionals tend to like abbreviations and acronyms. I don't know why. I can never remember what they stand for, but I'll include this one for the readers who like them.) The FFRP is the four words listed earlier. *Look. Listen. Love. And Let Go.* Let's add some depth to these main four ideas and learn how to do them.

STEP #1 LOOK INSIDE

Before dealing with the family friction happening outside of you, you must manage the conflict happening inside of you. That's right. You may not be in conflict with the other person, but you may be in conflict with yourself.

There are four primary diagnostic questions you want to ask at this stage. Then there are two prescriptive questions to ask later if you get the chance.

- What just happened?

- What am I thinking?

- What am I feeling?

- What am I going to do?

Question #1: What Just Happened?

The reality is that we never respond to reality; we respond to our perception of reality. Or to put it another way, we never respond to what happened; we respond to what we *think* happened. On one level, reality and perception are different. On a more practical level, perception *is* reality. Before you respond, you need to be clear on two questions: What do I think just happened? And Did what I think just happened actually happen?

Let's take the example of being disrespected by a family member. It happens. Think about the last time you felt disrespected by a family member. Who was it? What did they do or not do that made you feel disrespected? Got it? Okay. Let's try to take it apart.

The first thing you have to do is determine whether you are dealing with reality or your perception of reality. Did they really say that, or is that what you heard? Did they really do that, or is that what you think they did? You want your perception of what happened to match what actually happened. And it helps if your perception of what happened matches their perception of what happened.

For instance, when you text someone and you don't get a response—now you're angry, but you have no idea what happened. They could be busy. They may not be able to respond. They may have their phone off. They may have something else going on. But your mind will try to fill in the gaps. You are going to think you know what happened, but you may be responding to something that never actually happened.

Question #2: What Am I Thinking?

When you look at yourself first, and you're pretty sure you're responding to something that actually happened, the next thing you have to do is figure out what you are thinking.

You can think about your own thoughts, and you want to make peace with your own thoughts first. You know when your mind goes to a dark place that is not going to help you. And you need to back it up a little bit and say, "Hold on a minute, what am I thinking? I heard a person in recovery say, "And then you started thinking? When has that ever worked for you?" "I was on my way to go do the right thing, but then I started thinking." It is possible to think too much. You can think yourself into or out of bad situations. Negative thoughts produce negative emotions. Positive thoughts produce positive emotions.

Question #3: What Am I Feeling?

When it comes to managing friction, emotions may not be your friends. I'm not saying numb them because you don't want to numb your emotions. That goes bad in a hurry. You don't want to try to control emotions. You want to take them along for the ride. But you don't want to let them drive. If you let the emotions drive, they're going to put you into a ditch. You can feel angry, hurt, and frustrated, but venting those emotions in the middle of managing friction can often make the situation worse and create more friction.

What you want to do is move beyond the fight, flight, or freeze response and re-engage your rational brain. You want to get in touch with your values. What do you really care about?

What is important to you? What kind of person are you, and what kind of person do you want to be? Getting in touch with your morals, character, and values will give you much better guidance than your emotions. Once you have dealt with the conflict inside of you, you can start to deal with the friction outside of you. Now you can formulate and activate your best response to the situation.

Question #4: What Am I Going to Do?

Before you decide how you are going to respond and what you are going to do, there are a couple things you should be aware of. These are the two prescriptive questions I mentioned earlier.

Prescriptive Question #1: Am I being judgmental? If so, avoid the judgement trap.

The judgement trap sounds like this. "They did that because ..." That sentence is a trap. When I'm talking to someone in my office, I usually don't even let them finish the sentence. Most of the time we don't know why we do what we do. How are we possibly going to know why somebody else did what they did? Why are you reading this book right now? Can you clearly express what's motivating your behavior? Are they good motives? Are you trying to become a better parent, person, or family member? Are you doing it for others or for yourself? If you are doing it for yourself, is that essentially selfish? Is that okay? If judging our own motives is that complicated, what right do we have to judge the motives of others, and what possibility do we have of getting it right? It's best not to go there in the first place.

We still may be thinking or feeling, *Well, they shouldn't have done that. Here's what they should have done.* But you have to make a choice. You can love people, or you can judge them, but it's very difficult to do both at the same time. One of the things you find will find in this book is that there is a lot of love and not much judgement. "Did you just train wreck and relapse? Okay. We can handle that. We'll work on that. You're not going to get judged for that. That's part of the process."

You don't want to judge thoughts, motives, or attitudes. When the Bible says not to judge, that's what it's talking about. We do have to judge behavior, and most of us need to learn the process of dividing the two. You may not know the thoughts or the motives of the other person, but you do know what was said, and you know what was done. That's what you need to focus on. Focus on the behavior and not on judging the person. Focus on the behavior but also focus on maintaining the relationship.

Prescriptive Question #2: Am I overreacting? If so, know your triggers.

Triggers are when you have a big response to a small event. I'll give you one of mine—every time my son gives me "the sigh", it drives me nuts. It brings any violent tendencies I have right to the surface. Another one of mine is when I hear a parent tell a child to do something, and the child looks back and says, "No." That was not acceptable in the house I grew up in. I was not raised that way, so I have a very strong emotional reaction to it.

If you are feeling very strong emotions, it's possible that you've been triggered. Trigger events are small events that produce big reactions—like when you ask your teenager to do something and you get the eye roll, plus the sigh, plus the whining. Now you are triggered. You have all kinds of strong emotions going on inside of you that want to come out. Your teeth are clenched, your muscles are tense, your breathing is tense, and there are lots of thoughts swirling in your head that want to become words that will pour out of your mouth and destroy your child. You've taken that big inhale of oxygen that is going to fuel the attack. (It's not just me, is it?)

Let it out slowly. Remember, taking a deep breath and letting it out slowly is *Coping Skill #1*.

Everybody has triggers. And everybody who has a family has a family member who triggers them. You must learn what your triggers are and learn not to let them control you. Triggers can make you feel angry, frustrated, threatened, or some combination of the three.

These three emotional responses are related to two primary causes: desire and fear. Either you want something, and you are not getting it, or you're afraid of something and you are being threatened by it. We're not saying that your desire or fear is good or bad; we are only acknowledging it exists. As a parent, your desire can be that you want your child to be happy, successful, and independent. And what just happened indicates you are not going to get what you want. That's going to be a trigger. Or maybe you are afraid your child is going to make the same mistakes you made, experience the same pain you experienced, or die as a result of these mistakes or experiences. Any event that makes you face your fear is likely to be a trigger event. If you get triggered, that's on you. It's your responsibility to know your triggers and find ways to handle them.

Now you are ready to do something. But what should you do first?

STEP #2: LISTEN TO UNDERSTAND (COMMUNICATION)

You have looked at yourself first and gotten a handle on what is going on inside of you, but that's only half the battle. You have gained some clarity on your perspective, but now it's time to gain some clarity on the other person's perspective. You need to listen to them and what they are saying. This step is incredibly difficult for most people. But it's the most important step. It's the game-changer. The more understanding you have of a situation, the more appropriately you can respond to it.

The key to understanding is listening.

You want to take the time to let the other person tell their side of the story.

Be willing to ask for help with this. Ask them, "Help me understand what's going on inside of you. I don't know what you're thinking, tell me what you are thinking. I don't know what you are feeling, tell me what you are feeling. I don't understand where that behavior came from. I want you to tell me. I want to understand you." Isn't that what we all want? All of us want someone to take the time to understand us. That is the gift we can give. Ask the other person to help you understand what is going on. You won't know how to react or respond appropriately until you try to understand what is going on from the other person's perspective. You've looked inside yourself, now you want to try to catch a glimpse of what is happening inside the other person.

But what if they are unwilling to talk? What if they are triggered by you asking them questions? In that case, listen to their silence. Accept it. Share it. In the Bible, when Job's friends came to comfort him, they sat with him in silence for seven days before they spoke. Once they started speaking, they gave him a bunch of bad advice. Sometimes, it's better to sit in silence and not say anything. Wait for the other person to speak first. Then listen to what they have to say.

If they are open to you asking questions, ask them the four questions we asked ourselves when looking inside ourselves (pg 111). What happened? What are you thinking? What are you feeling? What are you going to do?

In Chapter 6, we talked about how important communication is for family development. Communication occurs when you share an understanding of the other person's situation. It occurs when you empower yourself to say, "So, what you're saying is this." And the other person says, "Yes, now you understand." That's the point you want to get to, but getting there requires somebody being willing to listen. Somebody must go first, and since you're now the one in control, you're going to take the lead. You are going to be the mature, responsible grown up. Sorry. It's a tough job, but somebody's got to do it.

When people say they want help, but they aren't willing to listen, I like to use the quote from the *Jerry Maguire* movie. "Help me help you." I want to help you, but you have to help me help you. It's a great line. Do you know the rest of the scene? The Rod Tidwell character says, "See, that's the difference between you and me. You think we're having an argument. I think we're finally starting to communicate." They are finally getting to the point where they're being honest, but it takes somebody willing to listen and understand.

STEP #3: LOVE UNCONDITIONALLY

"It's difficult to love the difficult, and it hurts to love the hurting."

In Chapter 2, we said unconditional acceptance and supportive relationships were two essentials in building a family. We said it's possible to separate the person from their behavior and accept the person without necessarily approving or accepting their behavior. We also said it was possible to separate the person from the decisions they make. It is possible to support the person without necessarily supporting every decision they make.

In this chapter, we want to look at the role love plays in helping us accept and manage family friction. When we love someone unconditionally, it means we accept them for who they are, not for who we want them to be.

Let me give an oversimplified definition of love.

"Love is a desire for good."

Self-love is a desire for good things for ourselves. Self-less love is a desire for good things for others. Our goal in looking inside is to get ourselves to the point that, however we decide to respond to family friction, our response is motivated by love.

To get there, we must avoid responding out of some negative emotions and desires.

1. **Anger.** Generally, we get angry when we want something, and we're not getting it. Family friction can produce anger when somebody wants something, and they are not getting it. It can be as simple as not being able to go where you want to go, leave when you want to leave, eat where you want to eat, do what you want to do, or achieve what you want to achieve. The other person is preventing you from getting what you want, and that makes you angry. It also makes you human. Anger itself is not bad. It becomes bad depending on what you do with it. When dealing with family friction, we will experience anger, but we don't want our words and actions to be a result of it. We generally tend to regret the things we say and do when we are angry.

2. **Revenge.** A desire for revenge is frequently a result of being hurt. What the other person said or did hurt you, and now you want to hurt them back. Again, this is a very normal, human response. Sometimes we think we are pursuing justice, but we unintentionally slip over the line into wanting revenge. The desire to return to others the harm they have done to us goes back to the beginning of human history. In Latin, it's *Lex talionis*. In the Bible, it's described as "an eye for an eye, a tooth for a tooth."

In responding to family friction, it's tempting to respond badly and justify it by an appeal to fairness. Children do it all the time. They cry, "That's not fair!" My response was this: "I'm not trying to be fair; I'm trying to be good." The expanded version was "Being fair would mean I treat you all the same.

But you are not the same, so if I treated you the same when you are not the same that wouldn't be fair or good. But if you want me to treat you exactly the same as I treat your brother or sister, I can, but I don't think that's what you want, and I don't think you'll like it."

They didn't like the expanded version very much.

3. **Unlived lives.** Carl Jung is well known for his quote, "The greatest burden a child must bear is the unlived life of the parent." I think that idea can be expanded to include the concept that the greatest burden a parent must bear is the unlived life of the child. As parents, we cannot live out our unlived lives through our children, and we cannot hold our children, or anybody for that matter, to the lives we expected them to live.

   The single greatest principle I can share with parents is this. Let go of the child you wanted; love the child you have. People in general—and children specifically—want to be loved and accepted for who they are, not who we think they ought to be or should be.

   Family friction is easier to manage when we have accepted ourselves and our own lives. When we accept ourselves, who we are, and the lives we live, it is easier to accept others, who they are, and the lives they live.

   The loving unconditionally step of looking inside brings us to the point where we've cleared ourselves of all motivations except one—love for the other person. However we decide to respond, and whatever the outcome of that decision, we want to be able to look back on it and honestly say, "I did what I did and said what I said out of love."

STEP #4: LET GO AND HOLD ON (HOPE)

"Love means knowing when to hold on and when to let go."

Step number four is about gaining the ability to let go of the desire to control the relationship without letting go of the relationship itself. It's about letting go of the desire to control the other person without giving up hope for them. It's about accepting the fact that we can't control anybody other than ourselves, and we can't control the outcomes of other people's decisions or behavior. It's about accepting the fact that most of life is out of our control most of the time.

As relationships grow and develop, they change.

In the parenting relationship, we want our children to move from dependence to independence, to interdependence.

"Parenting is the process of losing control of your children."

When you teach a child to walk, you start by holding on, but eventually, you have to let go. Then they fall. Then you pick them up again and repeat the process. The goal is to help them learn to walk, both away from you and toward you. Their choice. Then you put them on the school bus. You hold their hand, then you let it go. You teach them how to ride a bike. You hold on, then you let go. You teach them how to drive a car. You hold on (for dear life), then you let go and watch them drive away. This is successful parenting. It was summarized quite nicely in the movie, *Nanny McPhee.* "When you need me, you will not want me. When you want me, you will not need me." As parents, we ultimately want to be wanted but not needed.

In fostering this development, we willingly give up control and hope to exchange it for influence. One of the signs of a healthy relationship is when the other party is free to make their own decision, but they value your input enough to ask for it.

Let's try to apply the *Look-Listen-Love-Let Go* approach to a not uncommon real-life situation.

You just had an argument with your child. They gave you the sigh/grunt and the eye roll, said some mean things ("I hate you, you're the worst parent ever" kind of stuff) and went into their room and slammed the door. It's your move.

LOOK INSIDE

Your child is angry and frustrated. You are angry and frustrated. They are hurting. You are hurting. What do you do? Use *Coping Skill #1*. Take your deep breath and calm your emotions. Don't make it about you. If you can't make it better, at least don't make it worse. Don't return anger for anger. Don't return hurt for hurt. You can't be childish with your child—you have to be the grown up. You have to break the cycle. You cannot teach self-control by losing self-control. You cannot cure anger with more anger.

If you're like me, you may be asking yourself, "Do I knock down the door?"

Maybe.

But let's stop and think first.

You do not knock down the door out of anger. That's only going to produce more anger.

You do not knock down the door out of a desire to control the situation. That will probably only make the situation more difficult to control.

There may be a good reason to knock down the door. We'll get to that in a minute.

LISTEN TO UNDERSTAND

Again, you may have to allow for some silence before talking or asking questions. In trying to understand, we still want to gain answers to those same four questions.

- What happened?

- What are you thinking?

- What are you feeling?

- What are you going to do?

This is not a good time to give commands. Saying, "Open this door right now, or I'm going to break it down" may seem like a good idea. But asking, "Are you okay?" "What's going on?" Or "Could you open the door?" might get a better response. The goal is not to break down the door; the goal is to get them to open it.

LOVE UNCONDITIONALLY

This is where you want to rid yourself of all motivations but one. Whatever happens next, you want to be able to tell yourself you responded out of sincere desire to do what was best for your child, that you responded out of love. That is the one reason you might need to break the door down. Not out of anger, not out of a need to be controlling, but out of love. If you have reason to believe it is not safe for your child to be alone, you must go in, especially if they have a history of self-harm or self-destructive behavior.

You can approach it something like this.

- Can you talk to me and let me know you're okay?

- I'm just going to sit here until I know you're okay.

- I need for you to open the door and let me know you're alright.

If they give you enough of a response to let you know they are safe and not in immediate danger, then you can step back, take a moment, and figure out what your next response should be.

Remember, this doesn't have to be conflict, but it can be managed as friction.

11

RESPONDING TO FAMILY FRICTION

Now that we've made progress in accepting the reality of family friction, we can move forward and attempt to respond to it in a way that makes it better, not worse. We can respond to it in a way that is strong, healthy, and supportive.

There are four kinds of friction in the physical world: static, sliding, rolling, and fluid. I'm going to suggest that they correspond to four possible—and acceptable—responses for family friction.

Here are the four options:

1. Push back—Oppose and prevent   (static friction)

2. Let it slide—Allow and resist   (sliding friction)

3. Roll with it—Allow and assist   (rolling friction)

4. Embrace it—Agree and support   (fluid friction)

At the end, we will add a fifth response, which is the last resort when the other four don't work.

There is a story in the Bible that offers great insight into handling family friction. It's traditionally known as the story of The Prodigal Son. It can be found in the book of Luke, chapter 15, verses 11-32 (NIV). It is generally considered to be one of the greatest stories ever told.

For those unfamiliar with it, here it is.

There was a man who had two sons. The younger one said to his father, "Father, give me my share of the estate." So, he divided his property between them. Not long after that, the younger son got together all he had, set off for a distant country, and there squandered his wealth in wild living. After he had spent everything, there was a severe famine in that whole country, and he began to be in need. So, he went and hired himself out to a citizen of that country, who sent him to his fields to feed pigs. He longed to fill his stomach with the pods that the pigs were eating, but no one gave him anything.

When he came to his senses, he said, "How many of my father's hired servants have food to spare, and here I am starving to death! I will set out and go back to my father and say to him: Father, I have sinned against heaven and against you. I am no longer worthy to be called your son; make me like one of your hired servants." So, he got up and went to his father.

But while he was still a long way off, his father saw him and was filled with compassion for him; he ran to his son, threw his arms around him, and kissed him. The son said to him, "Father, I have sinned against heaven and against you. I am no longer worthy to be called your son."

But the father said to his servants, "Quick! Bring the best robe and put it on him. Put a ring on his finger and sandals on his feet. Bring the fattened calf and kill it. Let's have a feast and celebrate. For this son of mine was dead and is alive again; he was lost and is found." So, they began to celebrate.

Basically, what happens is that there is a very wealthy father. The father has two sons. The younger son tells his dad, "I wish you were dead. You have money, and I want my inheritance. I don't care about you. I do care about the money. Give me my inheritance now. I'm out of here." That's bad enough in our culture, but in their culture, it was unacceptable to disrespect your elders. That was some major family friction, but it wasn't because they were moving in different directions. They were moving in the same direction but at different speeds. Did the father want the son to have the inheritance? Yes. Did the father want the son to be happy? Yes. They weren't arguing about the outcome, they were arguing about how to get there and when to make it happen. The friction wasn't over *if* he would get the inheritance; the friction was about *when*. Let's look at how the father could have responded using the four options we have listed.

1. PUSH BACK—OPPOSE AND PREVENT

The push-back response is when you oppose and prevent. The father could have said, "No." He could have said, "I'm not giving you your inheritance, and you're not leaving." He could have called in the guards or police of his day and tried to prevent his son from leaving. He could have opposed and prevented, which is saying, "I do not give you permission, and I will try to stop you." Push back is an appropriate response when we see someone we love about to do something harmful, something that will have significant negative consequences. Push back is a loving response. It says, "Because I care about you, I am going to oppose what you are doing and try to prevent you from doing it." In any family relationship, particularly when there are mental health or recovery issues involved, pushing back can be the most loving response. It may be easier to say, "Go ahead, do what you want. I don't care. It's your life." But that's not loving. I told my kids, "I will always fight for you, which means sometimes I will fight with you." I heard the leader of a recovery group say, "We will help you live, but we will not help you die."

Sometimes, in managing friction, you are going to have to say no. That's not always a bad response. If you love somebody, and they are making bad decisions and bad choices, you have to make a decision. Are you going to sit passively and watch them self-destruct? Or are you going to get in the way? Sometimes you express love by setting limits and boundaries.

We often had to set limits with our own children. Once when my daughter was a teenager, she came out of her room wearing something that was not appropriate for school. Her mom and I looked at each other and said, "You're not wearing that to school. Go back and try again." She came out quickly wearing something different and said, "Okay, is this better?" It was. She had on her backpack, and she left out the door. As she left, my wife and I looked at each other. We both knew she had put that outfit in her backpack, and she was going to change when she got to school. That was a bad decision on her part. My wife looked at me and said, "I got this." She went to the school and waited for our daughter to get into her first class. Then she asked the principal if she could pull her daughter of class. The principal agreed, so Mom went to the classroom and knocked on the window. My daughter looked up and knew she was busted. That's pushing back. That's saying, "No, you're not going to do that. I'll take away the keys. I'll take away the car. I'll take away the phone. Remember, we cannot control other people or the consequences of their behavior, but sometimes love requires us to try. Pushing back is good and acceptable and the strongest response that you can have. But it's not the only response.

2. LET IT SLIDE—ALLOW AND RESIST

The father could have said, "You can leave, but I'm not giving you the money." Allow and resist is the appropriate response when you feel the other person is wrong or about to make a mistake, but you don't have the ability to stop them, and they are not open to your influence in trying to talk them out of it. It says, "I can't stop you, but I can't support you."

Usually, when you decide to let let it slide, you will also allow the other person to experience the consequences of their own behavior. You are not the one who is punishing them. You are allowing room for life, God, karma, or whatever you believe in to teach them that actions have consequences. We make our choices, and then our choices make us. There is such a thing as cause and effect. What goes around, comes around. If you constantly interfere with someone experiencing the consequences of their own behavior, they will eventually come to believe nothing they do matters. That can make them believe that they themselves don't matter. And eventually, nothing matters.

However, there are times when it is loving to step in and help soften the impact of some of those consequences. This is the world of grace, mercy, and forgiveness. When the consequences of the behavior are proportionate to the behavior itself—and temporary—allow the consequences to occur. Don't get in the way. Don't interfere. Small mistakes should result in small consequences. Bigger mistakes result in bigger consequences. But if the consequences are *not* proportionate to the behavior, or they are permanent and *not* temporary, then it is loving to get involved and even take some of the consequences yourself that were meant for the one you love. Small mistakes should not result in big, permanent, disproportionate consequences. Yes, sometimes it happens. But when it does, everybody seems to agree that it's unfair.

3. ROLL WITH IT—ALLOW AND ASSIST

This is the option the Father took. He allowed his son to go, and he gave him the money. Very often we choose this response when we don't support what the other person is doing, but we're not offended by it, and the risk and consequences are likely to be proportional and temporary.

Here's an example. My wife wanted to get a pool, but I didn't want to get a pool. So, we compromised and got a pool. At the time, I thought it was a mistake. I didn't think we should spend the money. I didn't think it was the right time. I didn't want the hassle of taking care of a pool. The decision caused some family friction. I ended up in the awkward position of not wanting have a pool but wanting her to have a pool. We're married, so if one of us got a pool, we both ended up with a pool. That's how marriage works. I knew how much she wanted one. I knew how happy it would make her. I knew how much she would enjoy having the grandkids come over to swim. I wanted her to be happy. Eventually, I made the choice to roll with it. I didn't oppose and prevent. I didn't oppose and resist and say, "If that's what you want, fine, but I'm not helping." I decided to allow and assist. Even though I didn't want it for myself, I wanted it for her. I helped and assisted her in getting it. Sometimes, that's what love does. Overtime, I think I'm going to learn to like having a pool.

4. EMBRACE IT—AGREE AND SUPPORT

When it comes to the story of the Prodigal Son, nobody ever thinks of this response. I've known that story for years, and I never thought of this option until recently. Embracing it is when you realize the other person is right, and you were being a jerk. It's not that big of an issue, and you were only saying no out of convenience. This is something you can say yes to, and it's not going to hurt anything. You actually change your position. The father could have said, "You know what? The eldest son wants the farm. I was thinking about retiring anyway. I think that since the younger son came in and asked for his inheritance, I'm just going to give the older son the farm now. It's all his. He wants it. He can have it. Run the farm, son, it's all yours. The younger son and I are going to go out and spend his inheritance." It was an option. It's a humble option of saying, "I picked the wrong battle. The other person was right. I'm going to apologize for making it difficult. I'm going to embrace what they want to do, and I'm going to support them in doing it". That will reduce the friction. That will get you someplace.

Embrace it is the response you give when you come around to the other persons way of thinking. Embrace it is when you realize the other person was right and you were wrong, and you want to help produce a positive outcome. You have the option of growing and changing, looking at things differently, and doing things you've never done before. It's possible for a parent to say to a child, "You were right; I was wrong. That was a great idea. I never would have thought of that. The new way is better than the old way. Let's do it your way."

If none of the other four options work, there is a fifth option, but it's the most severe. It's one way of managing family friction, but it comes at a high cost. It should not be the first option, and it should not be done unless none of the other options have been adequate to handle the situation.

5. SEPARATE—PROTECT AND DEFEND

Separation is when you have to remove contact with the other person so you can "protect and defend yourself and others from the consequences of the other persons behavior.

Sometimes family friction becomes unmanageable. It generates so much heat and is so abrasive that it threatens the viability of the entire family system. It is possible that the other person has no desire to help themselves, and they have the desire to hurt others. In these cases, the last resort is to separate.

It doesn't mean the person is not loved or cared for. Very often, the person who initiates the separation feels pain, remorse, regret, and guilt every day the separation exists. But they realize it is the only option left. Separation is necessary when the relationship carries a high risk of harm and no potential for benefit. It's when one person looks at another and says, "We're done." It acknowledges that we may lose them, but it also acknowledges they are already gone, and we no longer have them anyway.

Do you give up on hope for the person? No. Do you give up on hope for the relationship? No. Do you suspend the relationship? Yes. You allow the other person to be on their own by taking a step back.

Self-protection is ultimately job one. Think about how you try to save a drowning person. If you go out and try to rescue a drowning person, they are going to panic and try to push you under, and now you have two drowning people. Trying to save someone from quicksand? (More of a problem in the movies than in real life.) You don't get in the quicksand to help the other person out. Then you would have two people trapped in the quicksand. What about when the oxygen mask comes down on an airplane? What are the instructions? Put your own oxygen mask on first. If you pass out, you can't help anybody else. Self-protection is important if you are going to be around to lovingly help the person in the future.

A man in my church shared his recovery story with me. He told me he didn't start making progress in recovery until his family was done with him, and he was on his own. But then he also said that when he was finally in recovery, he called and thanked his father for never giving up hope. I think this is the right balance to work toward achieving, but it is a very difficult balance to maintain.

PART IV

How to Achieve Family Healing

12

FAMILY PAIN

"Psychological flexibility encourages patients to stop trying to control their pain and to embrace the fact that unpleasant experiences are a part of life."[1]

When I want to get to know someone, there's a request I can make that always gets a strong response. It might be a strong positive or negative response, but it's a strong response. The request is "tell me about your family." How does that sentence make you feel? Is your response something like, "Well, it's complicated?" I get a different response if I ask grandparents about their grandkids. If I ask grandparents about their grandkids, parents about their children, or children about their parents, those relationships are easier to articulate. But when I say, "Tell me about your family," I get this mix of "well ... it's ... uh ... it's complicated."

Some people want you to believe that the secret to happiness is family. All you have to do is get married, have kids, and you'll be happy." It's true that those things can make you happy. But what other feelings will they make you feel? Angry. Frustrated. Sleep deprived. Guilty. A lot of other feelings that are decidedly *not* happy. Family is a mixed blessing.

This brings us to the concept of family pain. Have you ever heard a doctor say, "Hold still, this is going to hurt a little?" Well, I'm saying it now. I'm going to let you know up front that you need to hold still, and this is going to hurt a little. One of my favorite quotes from one of my favorite movies is this. "Life is pain, highness. Anyone who tells you different is selling something." It's from *The Princess Bride*.

Think about it.

Life begins with labor and pain, and it never changes. Pain is the price of admission to life.

How do you know there's a new life coming into the world? Labor and pain. Can you achieve a life free of labor, pain, hard work, and discomfort? No. But is it still worth living? Yes.

The Nature of Emotional Pain

We have done pain management badly for decades. Somehow, from somewhere, we've gotten the idea that pain is unnatural and unnecessary. We've bought into the myth that you should always be happy, and you should never feel pain. But that's not how life works.

One of the reasons we have an opioid crisis is because we stressed pain avoidance rather than pain management. I remember once leaving a doctor's office after a minor outpatient surgery and being offered a prescription for Percocet. I wasn't in pain and didn't expect to be, but it was offered, just in case.

Life includes both physical and emotional pain. The vows I said when I got married ended with the words, "Till death do us part." Wait. What? Nobody explained that the best base scenario for a marriage is you stay together until one of you dies first, and the other tries to go on without the other. And the longer you are together, the harder it becomes for the one person to go on without the other. And that's the best case scenario. There are other ways for the marriage to end, but they are all harder and more painful. Gee, thanks.

If you've seen the movie, *UP*, you are familiar with the nine-minute love story at the beginning between Carl and Ellie. It ends with her dying. And that's how the movie *starts*.

In the movie, *Hitch*, Will Smith stars as the main character who helps people find love. In the movie, one of his clients finds love and then gets his heart broken. The dialogue goes like this.

> *Albert:* You know, honestly, I never knew I could feel like this. You know? I swear I'm ... I'm going out of my mind. It's like I want to throw myself off of every building in New York. I ... I see a cab, and I just wanna dive in front of it because then I'll stop thinking about her.
> *Alex "Hitch" Hitchens:* Look, you will. Just give it time.
> *Albert:* That's just it. I don't want to. I mean, I've waited my whole life to feel this miserable. I mean, and if this is the only way I can stay connected with her, then . . . well, this is who I have to be.

That's about accepting that life and love and relationships, even loving, family relationships, come with a certain amount of pain attached to them.

Accepting pain is part of life. Why? Because it's part of getting and having the things we want. I don't have any tattoos, but I hear that getting them is extremely painful. I suppose what happens is that people sign up to get a tattoo, find out it's extremely painful, and then never get another one, right? Nope. That's not how it works. People often start planning their next tattoo while getting their first one. Accepting and experiencing the pain is part of the process of getting a tattoo.

Consider these lyrics from the song "Believer" by Imagine Dragons.

"I was broken from a young age

Taking my sulking to the masses

Write down my poems for the few

That looked at me, took to me, shook to me, feeling me

Singing from heartache from the pain

Taking my message from the veins

Speaking my lesson from the brain

Seeing the beauty through the (pain)

You made me a, you made me a believer, believer

(Pain, pain)

You break me down, you build me up, believer, believer

(Pain)

Oh let the bullets fly, oh let them rain

My life, my love, my drive, it came from

(Pain)"

Many of the best things in life come after accepting and working through painful situations and events.

THE NATURE OF EMOTIONAL HEALING

Finding healing from emotional family pain can be a long, difficult process. Emotional pain has more in common with physical pain than we think. Let me give you an example. When I was about ten years old, I had the Achilles tendon on my right leg severed. We were taking rides in a line of little red wagons tied behind a riding lawn mower. Some of us older kids were jumping from one little wagon to the other. I missed. My right foot went down between the wagons and the front of one of the wagons punctured the back of my heel. It didn't sever a major nerve or artery, so it didn't really hurt or bleed that much. I limped back to the house to show the adults what had happened. They insisted we go to the emergency room.

At the emergency room, the doctor placed his hand under my knee and elevated my leg. "Raise your foot," he said. My brain understood the message and sent the appropriate response down to my foot. "Foot up." But my foot didn't respond. It didn't go up. I was very confused. Why wasn't my foot working? It was the first indication I had that something may be seriously wrong.

How do we know when our emotions are injured? They lose their function. They don't work right. We have ideas that we should be happy, sad, or excited, and we look for the appropriate emotions to respond, and they stare back at us with blank expressions as if to say, "I got nothing."

Back in the emergency room, the doctor said I had to go in for surgery as soon as possible. Tendons (and emotions) tend to shrink and retract when they are injured and out of use. I don't remember anything about the surgery because they knocked me out for that part of the healing process. Reattaching tendons (and emotions) is very painful. And in the surgery (like with emotions) there was some cutting involved. By the time I woke up the surgery was completed. They sent me home with a cast and a prescription for some pain medication.

Why did they send me home? Because the healing was going to be a long process. Why did they put me in a cast? Because my leg had recently been injured, the repair was fresh, and my leg needed to be immobilized. Why the prescription for pain meds? Because I was going to be in a lot of pain (duh). This is also how emotional healing works. A good therapist will help you reconnect with your emotions. This will be painful. Unfortunately, you can't respond well in therapy if you are sedated and unconscious. With emotional surgery, you must feel the pain. You may cry a little. Or a lot. It's okay.

Then you go home and start the healing process. You may want to immobilize the injured emotions for a while. They are still weak and bruised, and you may want to limit their use until they are stronger. The only way for them to get stronger is to start using them and stretching them. When I injured my leg, my physical therapist was my dad. Have I mentioned that my dad was a Marine? They are not known for being emotionally sympathetic. My dad determined that his son was going to regain full use of his leg. We had some pretty intense and painful therapy sessions. But it worked. My leg is healed, and it works fine now. It's healed.

Your injured emotions will have to go through a similar healing process. For severe emotional injury, I highly recommend getting a therapist. You may be able to get by with the support and helpful advice of friends and family, but sometimes, you need to pay a professional. Depending on what you're dealing with, you may need some medication to help with the healing. Don't shame yourself for needing pain meds or psych meds. If they are prescribed, take them. If you heal to the point where you can function without them, work with your doctor on a plan to decrease and eventually eliminate them. Don't abuse them. And don't stop taking them on your own. That doesn't ever go well. If you have a good therapist, appropriate medication, and support from friends and family, your prognosis for emotional healing is excellent.

But let me explain what I mean by healing. Let's go back to my leg injury. That wound was inflicted over forty years ago. Do I still have a scar? Yes. Does my leg work like it's supposed to? Yes. Can I dance? No, but that has nothing to do with the leg injury. I just can't dance. Does the old wound hurt sometimes depending on the weather? Yes. When I get tired, do I limp? Yes, a little. Is the leg exactly the same as it would have been if it had never been injured? No. But it's fully healed. That's also how emotional healing works. Emotions heal, but they usually leave scars. Sometimes they still hurt, depending on what's going on around you. Sometimes they cause you to limp through life a little, especially when you are tired. But they do heal.

To review, here is the sequence of events that make up the healing process for both physical and emotional injuries.
Trauma—Assess the damage. The ER question: What happened?
Shock—Manage the Pain. How much does it hurt? (On a scale of 1-10.)
Surgery— Repair the damage. Treat the Wound.
Immobilization—Cover and protect the wound.
Therapy—Regain use. Sometimes the therapy can be more painful than the initial injury.
Time—Have patience and persistence. Balance working and waiting.
Acceptance—Accept the reality of scars.

After an injury, things can be good again. Sometimes, they can even be better. But they can never be the same as they were before.

13

FAMILY GUILT

WHAT IS GUILT?

Not all guilt is the same. Guilt can vary by degrees. Consider the following questions and answers

- Did you eat my cookie? Guilty.

- Did you take money out of my wallet? Guilty.

- Did you kill them? Guilty.

TRANSGRESSIVE GUILT— CROSSING THE LINE OF RIGHT AND WRONG

In Western culture, two primary comprehensions of guilt exist. They are used interchangeably, but they are actually very different. Both are problematic, but in very different ways.

The first idea associated with guilt is the idea of a transgression. It comes from the Greek word *parabasis*. It literally means to step over the line. It is associated with laws, rules, and boundaries. Have you ever done or said something and then thought, *That was over the line?* That's the idea behind a transgression. In Chapter 7, we talked about the importance of boundaries in building a family. All relationships in all societies have some idea of boundaries. And when they are crossed, that's a transgression.

Guilt is a response to the idea that we have done something wrong, that we have violated a rule or boundary. Two sets of moral boundaries must be considered—internal boundaries and external boundaries. Internal boundaries are our own set of morals and values. External boundaries are standards of morals and values set by others. In dealing with guilt, we must first consider what boundaries have been crossed, what wrong has been done. We must ask, have we violated internal standards (our own), external standards (societal standards), or both.

EXPECTATIVE GUILT—FAILING TO MEET EXPECTATIONS

The second idea is related to the Greek word *amartia*. Originally an archery term, it's referred to as missing the bull's eye. Metaphorically, it was about not being perfect. For us, it's the guilt we feel from missing expectations. This is the source of the guilt we explain by using phrases like, "I should have," or "I shouldn't have." It's what we feel when we disappoint or hurt someone. It's not a transgression of a law, but it's the sacrifice of a principle or value.

Where does guilt come from? There are two sources of guilt.

THE GUILT WE RECEIVE

Transgressive guilt and expectative guilt can be self-imposed or imposed on us by others. In Chapter 14, we will lay out a process for dealing with guilt and restoring relationships. The process is the same whether the source of the guilt is ourselves or someone else, but the application of the process is different.

THE GUILT WE GIVE

It isn't often that I think of myself as the source of someone else's guilt. I don't usually get asked, "Are you trying to make me feel guilty?" But if I'm honest with myself, the answer would probably be "yes." I have tried to make people feel guilty in the past.

There are two ways guilt is used (or even weaponized) in family relationships.

Sometimes guilt is used for manipulation, which is simply a way of maintaining control over someone. It's also known as guilt-tripping. Passive aggressive guilt-tripping is pervasive in some families. You know how it feels when someone is trying to control or manipulate you through guilt. It doesn't feel good. It builds resentment. So, just decide right now that you are going to take this nasty little tool out of your toolbox and never use it again. Remember, we want to influence the people in our families, not control them.

Sometimes guilt can be used as punishment. It's the parent saying to the child, "I want you to sit there and think about what you've done." Or, "Do you know how badly you hurt me?" Here's the thing. Guilt is a form of punishment, but only when it's self-imposed. It should not be given as a punishment. To build strong, healthy, supportive relationships, we must work to remove guilt, not create it.

HOW DO I DEAL WITH IT?

How you deal with the guilt depends on what context the transgression occurred or in what area expectations were not met. Guilt generally occurs in three contexts—historical, legal, and emotional.

HISTORICAL GUILT

Historical guilt, obviously enough, is when the guilt is a matter of history. It answers the question, "Did you do it, or did you not? Are you, or are you not guilty? Did it happen, or didn't it? This is important to consider because sometimes we feel guilty for things that never happened. And sometimes things happen that we are not aware of, and we only feel guilt when we find out about them.

When it comes to dealing with historical guilt, the only thing you can do is accept it. Yes, I did that. Yes, that happened. One of the rules of mental health is that you can't change the past. You can change your understanding or perspective on it, but you can't undo it.

LEGAL GUILT

As anyone who has worked with our legal system knows, there is a difference between historical guilt and legal guilt. It is possible to be historically guilty (you did it) but have the court declare you not guilty. And it is possible to not be historically guilty and have the court find you guilty. Humans courts are necessary, but they are not infallible.

What can you do when you are dealing with the issue of legal guilt? I'm not a lawyer, and I don't pretend to give legal advice. But I can lay out a principle that I think is helpful. Here it is: you can work the system, and you can work to change the system. Working the system means be smart. Get the best advice you can and get all the help you can. Figure out how the system works and use it to try to procure just, fair, and equitable outcomes.

But understand the system is flawed and imperfect because the people who make it up are flawed and imperfect. We must constantly work to change the system. And by that, I don't mean destroy it, I mean work to make it better.

Emotional Guilt

Emotional guilt is the guilt we feel. It is also very different from historical and legal guilt. I can be historically guilty, which means I did it. I can be found guilty, which means they can prove I did it, but I may not feel any emotional guilt. I may not feel like I did anything wrong. I can be historically not guilty (I didn't do it), found legally not guilty (they couldn't prove I did it), and still have emotional guilt, which means I don't feel good about what happened.

Let me give you an illustration. In the small Ohio town that I used to live in, there was a speed trap. It was on the downhill side of a traffic light, and the speed limit suddenly dropped from thirty-five to twenty-five mph. At any given time of day, a police cruiser could sit there and write as many speeding tickets as he wanted to write. Unless you knew the trap was there and conscientiously hit your brakes, you were going to be over the speed limit. One day, it was my turn. I got stopped for doing thirty-six in a twenty-five mph zone. The officer pulled me over, wrote me a ticket, and let me go.

Was I historically guilty? Yes. I was going over the speed limit. Was I legally guilty? Yes, he saw me and had me on the radar. He had proof of my guilt. Did I feel guilty? *No.* I was driving safely at a reasonable speed. I thought the speed trap was ridiculous. I didn't speed through it on purpose or out of spite, but I didn't feel any guilt at all over my behavior. Did I pay the ticket? Yes, I did. I could have tried to fight it or mounted a campaign to get the speed trap removed, but I decided to work within the system, pay my fine, and get on with my life.

In summary, guilt is toxic in relationships. Even self-imposed emotional guilt can affect our behavior toward others. For strong, healthy, supportive relationships to survive, there must be a way of removing and healing guilt.

14

FAMILY RESTORATION

I love old furniture, especially when it has been carefully restored. It retains its original identity as well as the marks of age and the beauty of being renewed. It's called *patina*. Relationships that have been restored and transformed have a certain patina to them, and it's beautiful. Relationships that have worked through seasons of guilt and pain have a special quality to them. Time adds value to healthy relationships As the saying goes,

> *"Make new friends but keep the old, one is silver, the other is gold."*

We've talked about the healing process for emotional pain, but what is the process for getting rid of guilt? We have three institutional systems that tend to focus on producing and managing guilt: courts, families, and religion. The courts and most religious systems have produced ways to deal with the problem of guilt. We can apply concepts from both systems to create a way of dealing with guilt in family systems.

However, before moving ahead with attempting to heal and restore damaged family relationships, there are few things you should be aware of.

1. SOME RELATIONSHIPS CANNOT BE HEALED.

They just can't. When my kids were little, they would bring me toys and ask, "Daddy, can you fix this?" Sometimes I could. I'd say, "Yes, we can put that back together, glue it, and it will be fine." And sometimes, I would look at the toy and have to say, "No, I can't fix it. It's too badly broken. There are too many pieces missing. I don't have the skill." Relationships can work the same way. You want them to be restored and repaired. You want them to be healthy again. But the damage is too great. And you have to let them go.

For a relationship to be healed and restored, both parties have to be willing to participate in the process. It is possible that you may want to restore the relationship and the other person, for their own reasons, is unwilling. Or it's possible that someone wants to restore their relationship with you, and you, for reasons you may or may not fully understand, are unwilling. In either case, the relationship can't be restored. It's better to attempt to move on or let time pass before trying to put things back together.

2. SOME RELATIONSHIPS SHOULD NOT BE HEALED.

If it's toxic, unhealthy, or abusive, it should not be restored. This is usually easier to see in other people than it is in ourselves. You ask a friend , "Really, you're back with them? Why are you back with them? You know what's going to happen." And then they reply, "Well, you know, they said the right things, and then they did this, and it's going to be different this time." You want to scream, "No, it's not!" It's very hard to see when we are the ones doing it. When people tell me they want to repair a relationship, I have to ask if they are sure it's a good idea. It may be one of those relationships where restoring it is not going to do them any good, and it won't be good for the other person either.

You want to repair the relationships with people who bring out the best in you, not people who bring out the worst in you. When you don't even like yourself when you are with a person, you have to be careful. Maybe you shouldn't repair that one. There are those people who every time you get in trouble, you are with them. You might not want to repair that relationship.

Some relationships are so badly broken, wounded, and painful that restoring them would cause further injury to one or both parties. In such cases, it is best to accept the relationship for what it was and leave it in the past without trying to bring it into the present or future.

There's a verse in the Bible that says, "If possible, as far as it is up to you, live at peace with everybody." (Romans 12:18) This includes family members. But sometimes we must accept that the ability to live in peace with this person is not up to us.

If you conclude the relationship can be restored, and that it should be restored, here is a process that you can follow that will help. It draws from language used in courts, various churches, and twelve-step programs.

RESTORING A RELATIONSHIP IS A CRAFT

1. **C**onfession—Admit what you have done. Own your stuff.

The scenario frequently looks like this. There has been some silence between you and somebody else because of some things that have happened. You know you will have to talk to that person, and you know you are the person who screwed up. You said some things, and you did some things that were not okay, but you want that person to stay in your life. You want the relationship to continue. Where do you start? You start with confession. Admit what you have done. Own your stuff.

Here's what many people try to do. When they are trying to repair relationships, they start with *you* statements. They say something like, "I did this because you did that. And I think if you do this, and if you do that, then I think we can make it work." Then the other person says, "Why is this my fault? Why do I have to make all the changes?" Have you ever had that done to you, where the other person tries to repair the relationship, but they want you to do all the work? That's not a very appealing offer.

Confessing is not blame-shifting. It's not saying, "I did this because you did that." Confessing is not explaining. It's not saying, "I did this because …" Confessing is not excusing. It's not saying, "Yes, I did that, but it's not a big deal because …" Confessing is being honest. Confessing is pleading guilty. Confessing is taking responsibility for your actions.

When somebody comes to you and says, "Look. This is what I did, and I'm sorry." At least they are admitting it. At least they are being honest. When you say to someone, "I was wrong. That was my fault, and I'm sorry," you will most likely get a hearing.

There are two kinds of confessions: pre-discovery and post-discovery. Pre-discovery confession is when you are being honest about what you've done before it was discovered and before a crisis. Post-discovery confession is when you are being honest about what you've done after it was discovered or after a crisis.

I grew up in a small town that had one major employer. It was not an easy place for keeping secrets. Sometimes, Dad would come home from work and ask, "What did you do today?" or the dreaded, "Is there something you want to tell me?" This was my opportunity for confession.

The temptation was to try to figure out what he already knew and confess to that without confessing to something he didn't know about yet. As Jeff Foxworthy once said about being interrogated by the police or your wife, "Keep your hands on the wheel, look straight ahead, and give simple yes or no answers till you find out what you're being accused of. No sense confessing to something they don't know about yet."

The better response was to think this: *If I have something to confess, now is the best time to do it. Now is a good time to be honest and a really bad time to lie.*

But here's the thing to remember about confession. Have you heard that confession is good for the soul? Sure, it is, but it's also bad for the reputation. Should you tell everything all the time to everybody?

No, probably not. Too much information (TMI) is a real thing. When you share a confession with someone, you are not usually doing them a favor. You are asking them to carry a burden. They must now live with knowing what you confessed. It's good to ask yourself, "Does this person need to know this?"

There's a very helpful three-part confession test found in the Bible. Ephesians 4:29 tells us we shouldn't let corrupting, unwholesome speech come out of our mouths. This kind of speech is the opposite of good and wholesome speech. And it tells us to simply not let it come out of our mouths.

However, the verse offers a three-part exception clause. "Except as is good for edification, according to the need of the moment, that it may give grace to those who hear." Before sharing your confession, you should ask yourself three questions:

1. Am I building up or tearing down? Sometimes you must talk about some stinky, smelly, ugly, negative stuff in order to build up another person or restore the relationship. If the purpose is to build up and not tear down or destroy, then it's good to share it.

2. Is it necessary? Everything you say should be true, but that doesn't mean you have to say everything that's true. As the saying goes, "People who enjoy being brutally honest are usually more brutal than honest." Do not use the truth as a weapon to hurt others.

3. Will it benefit the person to whom you're confessing it? It's not especially loving or kind to tell a person something because you have to tell someone. There are supportive friends and family members who are up to that task, and you can unburden yourself to them. But in repairing a relationship, you must keep the thoughts, feelings, and well-being of the other person in mind. You can't make it all about you. If you are talking with someone who loves you, cares about you, and is trying to help you, then yes, it's helpful to them. It may make them angry, and it may hurt or disappoint them, but it's helpful to them in trying to restore the relationship. Ask yourself this question. Will they say, "Thank you for sharing that with me?"

So, before starting your confession, you need to be convinced that sharing what you want to share will build the other person up, it is necessary to share it, and in the long run, it will benefit the other person to hear it.

There's one more filter you can use to help you decide what you need to share. I call it the "right time, right place, right person" test. Before you share anything, ask yourself, "Is this the right time, right place, and the right person to share it with?" If it's not all three, then you might want to reconsider opening up and giving full disclosure of your life.

But what if you decide not to share it? Then what happens? Here's the principle.

What You Hide, You Get to Keep.

If you have a secret that is killing you, you are going to have to tell somebody about it. You are going to have to get it out. If you decide to hide it or lie about it, then it's yours. You're stuck with it. You have to keep it. As they say in recovery circles, "You are only as strong as your secrets."

But if you are hiding or lying about anything, then it is your burden and your responsibility. If you lie about it or hide it, you are stuck with it. Whatever it is you are lying about, whatever it is you are hiding, nobody can help you with that. If you want to be free of it, you are going to have to open up and put all the cards on the table and tell someone.

But what if it's too much for the other person, and they walk away? Then let them walk away. According to Madea, one of the big problems in life is when you try to hold onto people who are trying to leave. Some people are only meant to be in your life for a season. And you have to let them go.

2. **R**epentance—Change something or identify something that has already changed.

Repentance has to do with change. It can be a change in thinking or a change in behavior. When you are working to restore a relationship, the offended party wants to know that something is going to change—especially if this isn't the first time you've made this particular confession. You want to give them hope for change. And remember, "If nothing changes, everything stays the same."

As clearly as possible, you want to be able to state what is different. A change in thinking can be stated as, "I used to think that, but now I think this." A change in behavior can be indicated by saying, "I used to do this, but I'm not going to do that anymore. Now I'm going to do this. I never used to do this, but now I am doing it."

However, remember these are only words, and words are not always the best indicators of a changed reality. Many people over-promise and under-deliver. For years, I've heard people swear they've changed, and you know while they're talking they haven't. People who have really changed under-promise and over deliver.

Getting someone to believe you've changed takes time. I normally suggest you watch a person for a year before believing they've changed as much as they think they have. That's right. Twelve months. Four seasons. Expect to hear, "You say you've changed—prove it." That is why the next step is necessary.

3. Atonement—Do something to make it better.

When we think of atonement, especially us guys, we often think about flowers and chocolate. I once went to the store to buy some flowers for my wife. It was not an atonement situation, but the cashier looked at me, smiled and asked, "So, what did you do?" I smiled back and said, "I married a woman who likes flowers."

In 2003, Kobe Bryant seriously screwed up his marriage. Yet, as of this writing in 2019, he and his wife, Vanessa, are still together and expecting their fourth child. I don't know exactly what he did or what he confessed to, but everybody at the time knew about his alleged atonement. It was an 8-carat purple diamond with an estimated worth of four million dollars! I can only imagine the conversation.

Kobe: What can I do to make it up to you and show you I want to make this work?

Vanessa: I know just the thing.

The important part about atonement is this. The offended party gets to determine what it is. The offended party gets to answer the question, "What can I do make it up to you and demonstrate my sincerity?" The offender then must meet the obligation. Atonement works almost like a court sentence, except the purpose is not punishment, its purpose is restoration. The purpose of atonement is to prove someone's sincerity in their apology and their commitment to making things better. It doesn't have to be a gift. It can be discontinuing a relationship, getting rid of an item, keeping a promise, or finishing a task.

Atonement is different than doing penance. Penance helps the offender work off his own guilt while atonement helps the offender deal with the guilt in the relationship with the offended party.

4. Forgiveness—Attempt to give and receive forgiveness.

Chapter 15 will be all about forgiveness, but I want to introduce some basic ideas here. Atonement and forgiveness are not opposites, but they work together in the restoration process. The purpose of atonement is to help achieve forgiveness.

The offender is the one who needs to take the initiative and *ask* for forgiveness. Asking for forgiveness is different than giving an apology. In its classical usage, an apology is actually an explanation of a behavior and expression of regret. It's when you say, "I'm sorry." But as we all know, that doesn't always fix or change things.

Asking for forgiveness makes you vulnerable. The other person can always say no. They can be offended that you would even ask. The other person can reject your efforts to restore the relationship, and that can really hurt.

What if they do say no? It hurts as much as anything you will ever experience, and you have to find a way to deal with that. Rejection is emotionally painful. It's a fresh wound, but it will heal. Sometimes you have to ask the question in order to know what the outcome will be.

That's how it works. If you want to restore the relationship, you take the risk. You open yourself up to hurt, pain, and rejection. But you also open yourself up to healing and restoration.

5. Transformation - Find a way to bring good out of the bad. This is also called redemption.

Everybody likes a good redemption story. Movies that feature redemption stories include *Les Miserable, The Count of Monte Cristo, The Green Mile, It's a Wonderful Life, Groundhog Day, Gran Tourino,* and of course, *The Shawshank Redemption.* Redemption is the process of transformation.

Transformation is not the effort to make a bad thing into a good thing. I don't think that is always possible. Sometimes a bad thing is simply a bad thing. Transformation is the effort to bring a good thing out of a bad thing. I know there are phoenixes that rise out of the flame, and things that were once wounded or dead can come back to life and become new. Caterpillars can become butterflies. I know these things happen. What you are going to look for is the opportunity to transform what you have done or the things that have happened to you. You've confessed it. You've changed something. You've done something to make it better. You've asked for forgiveness. Now it's time to move on and try to bring something good out of it.

Lorrie and I have been together for thirty-five years. We've been through some hard times, made mistakes, and had to give and receive forgiveness. But we've always been able to take the broken pieces and put them back together. Now, what we have is better and stronger than it was before. We've faced our issues, and the strength we have now is the result of working through the obstacles we've encountered.

The bad times didn't make the relationship good. Getting through the bad times made it good. The bad times didn't produce the strength, depth, and sweetness in our relationship. Those things were produced by staying together and working to make things good, even when they were bad.

At the end of restoration process, after the confession, repentance, atonement, forgiveness, and transformation, you enter into a different kind of relationship. The ancient Greeks had a term for love relationships that had survived the test of time. The term *pragma* can mean "the practical love that endures." This is the kind of love that marks relationships that have survived and endured. It's one of the best kinds of love you can experience.

When I was a kid in high school, I had this old rocking chair in my bedroom. The original shellac finish had darkened and cracked. The woven cane back and seat had disintegrated, and I had to put a blanket over it so I could sit on it without falling through. It had been handed down to me from my great uncle and aunt's house. I didn't have a lot of family keepsakes, and I was emotionally attached to it, so I kept it.

In 1982, Lorrie came home with me from college to meet my parents for the first time. It was Christmas, and I wanted to give her a special present. I took that old rocking chair and restored it. I stripped off the old shellac, sanded it down, and gave it a new, natural, hand-rubbed finish. I spent what seemed like a lot of money at the time to have someone replace the woven cane back and seat. It looked beautiful, better than new. It was an unconventional Christmas present to give to a girlfriend who would soon become a fiancé.

Thirty-five years, four children, and four grandchildren later, that chair still sits in the corner of our bedroom under a pile of pillows and blankets. I really like those new rocking chairs they have out on the front porch of every Cracker Barrel in the country. They are well-crafted and made out of good wood. In truth, they are more solid and more comfortable than that old rocker in our bedroom. I bought one of those new Cracker Barrel rocking chairs for my daughter, and she used it when her kids were little. Now, it's sitting in my parent's house. It's a good chair, but it will never have greater value than the one that was restored .

15

FAMILY FORGIVENESS

"Forgiveness is the currency of long-term relationships."

Now, let's go deeper into how forgiveness works. We want it. We need it. But there's a lot of misconceptions about forgiveness. If you are going to be in a relationship with anybody—friend, co-worker, family, parent, child,—you are going to need to know how to forgive. Many of us don't how, and we're not good at it.

My daughter had brought my grandson over to the house to play one day. My wife and I were playing with him, enjoying being with him, and essentially letting him do whatever he wanted. We weren't saying no to anything. I don't remember specifically what it was, but we let him do something my daughter, his mom, didn't approve of. And she let us know.

She said we needed to be stricter with him and tell him no. I was offended! And before I thought about it, I said the following sentence, "Really? After all the stuff you put us through when you were in high school, you're going to tell us how to raise kids?" Oops. Not a smart thing to say. But my daughter very wisely responded, "Dad, if you want me to keep bringing the kids over to play, you're going to have to let go of all the stupid stuff I did in high school."

She was right. I had some unforgiveness issues I was holding onto. I told her I could do that if she would agree to stop bringing up some of the bad parenting decisions I had made while she was growing up. She agreed. We both were able to let go of the past and focus on building the relationship we wanted to have in the future. That's forgiveness. That's how it works.

The misconceptions about forgiveness make forgiving difficult and at times make it seem undesirable. Let's look at some of these forgiveness fallacies and then correct them with forgiveness insights.

FORGIVENESS FALLACY #1: FORGIVING IS NOT THE SAME AS FORGETTING

"You need to forgive and forget." This is the advice often given by well-meaning friends and family, but that's not how it works. Often, it's not even possible. Some things can never be forgotten. When you commit to the path of forgiveness, it doesn't mean making a commitment to forget all about it. You may or may not forget about the event or the behavior that requires forgiveness, but forgiving is a separate process and must be pursued separately.

FORGIVENESS FALLACY #2: FORGIVING IS NOT THE SAME AS TRUSTING

When trust has been broken, there is often a need for forgiveness to be applied to the situation, but forgiving and trusting are different issues. They are related, but they are not identical. The decision to forgive someone is different than the decision to trust them. Suppose my son asks to borrow my car, and I tell him no. After I leave, he takes it anyway and is involved in an accident. I may forgive him, with all that involves, but trust has been broken and must be restored separately. Forgiveness is given; trust is earned.

Most parents go through a stage of innocence with their children in which they think, *Oh, my child would never lie to me.* They trust their children and give them the benefit of the doubt. Then slowly, piece by piece, that innocence is eroded as the parent learns their child isn't as perfect as they'd like them to be. They may lie, they may hide things, or they may try to deceive their parents. This loss of innocence takes its toll on the parent, and it cannot be restored once it's lost. Should you forgive your child? For reasons that we will see later, yes. Should you trust your child? That depends on the child.

FORGIVENESS FALLACY #3 FORGIVING IS NOT THE SAME AS HEALING

When we form loving relationships with others, we risk getting emotionally injured, especially when it comes to our own children. Parents and children hurt each other. We inflict emotional wounds on each, sometimes accidently, sometimes on purpose. These wounds need to heal. Giving and receiving forgiveness is part of the healing process, but it isn't identical to the healing process. The two processes are related, and while they may happen concurrently, they aren't synonymous. Lack of forgiveness hinders the emotional healing process. For healing to occur, forgiveness must be pursued, or it should at least be allowed for.

The reality of forgiveness is that it has a short-term and a long-term dimension. It's both a decision, a choice if you prefer, and a process.

FORGIVENESS INSIGHT #1 FORGIVING IS ALWAYS A CHOICE

No one can ever be forced or required to forgive another person. It must be voluntary. It must be chosen. If you have been wronged or hurt by another person, the idea of forgiveness is usually met with some resistance. *Why should I forgive that person after what they did to me?* That is the right question to ask. You don't have to forgive them, though. Many people start their journey toward forgiveness from a very dark angry place. You might think, *Forgive them? No way. I'd rather watch them die a slow, painful death, attend their funeral only so I can go spit on their grave.* You never have to forgive anybody. Nobody can make you do it if you don't want to. There's always an alternative.

What is the alternative to forgiveness? Bitterness. Have you ever met a bitter person, someone who's angry at life, themselves, the world, and everything in it? Have you ever looked at an old person sitting on their front porch yelling at the neighbor kids to get off their lawn and wondered, *How did they get there?* Frequently, the answer is forgiveness. At one time in my life, I did a fair amount of end of life care. I've seen older people who knew they were dying refuse to see a family who had come at the end to say goodbye. They said, "I told that SOB that I would never forgive him as long as I live. And I'm not dead yet, so tell him to go away." That's the bitterness of unforgiveness. I have seen people not talk to each other for decades, even though they go to the same church, where they should know better.

And then there's unforgiveness in families, which may produce the greatest bitterness of all. Parents, children, siblings, husbands, and wives all say and do hurtful things. All make mistakes. All are insensitive, thoughtless, and selfish. That is why family forgiveness is so important. In my own family, there are branches of the family tree who haven't spoken to each other in generations. In some cases, they know why, but in other cases, they have no idea. What a loss and a shame.

FORGIVENESS INSIGHT #2 FORGIVING IS A PROCESS

When you see the only alternative to forgiveness is bitterness, it may start to gain some appeal as a viable option. But there's another obstacle. *Maybe I should forgive them,* you think, *but I'm not sure I can.* That's progress. You've already reached stage one of the forgiveness process.

FORGIVENESS INSIGHT #3 FORGIVING IS A SKILL

It is something you can practice. With time and practice, you can get better at it. Some people seem to be naturally good at forgiving while others may struggle with it. It's easier for some people than others. This could be a result of their personality type or the way they were raised. But everybody can improve their ability to forgive. The more you practice it, the better you get at it.

Here is how forgiving works. These are the stages you go through when you are in the process of forgiving someone.

STAGE 1: FINDING THE DESIRE TO FORGIVE

Here's how this one usually works. When we initially start thinking about forgiveness, the thought is *Hell, no. I don't want to forgive that person. I want them to suffer. And I want to watch. And then I want them to die a slow painful death. And I want to watch. And then I want them to rot for eternity in hell. That's what I want.*

It's okay if that's where you're at. You're at the beginning of the process. You don't ever have to forgive anybody. Like we said, it's always a choice. You can hold on to the anger and resentment if you want to. You can stay on the path of unforgiveness until it takes you to the place of bitterness. But why would you want to?

The desire to forgive does not come from wanting to do something that benefits the person you are forgiving. Let's be realistic. The person you are forgiving does not deserve to be forgiven. That's the whole point of forgiveness. If the other person got what they deserved, that would be considered justice. You don't offer forgiveness for the benefit of the other person, you offer forgiveness to the other person for your own benefit. You forgive them to find your own healing. Anger and bitterness are toxic, and as long as you hold on to them, they will poison you from the inside. The event you are forgiving is like the splinter that caused a wound. Left untreated, the splinter is likely to cause an infection, which will cause the initial injury to become inflamed and more painful. The only way for the wound to heal is to get the splinter out and treat the infection. Forgiveness is how you get the other's person's injurious activity out of your life so you can pursue your own healing.

You forgive to find your own freedom. Imagine you are walking down the sidewalk, and you see someone who hurt you walking toward you. You are still hurt and angry at that person, and you change your path to avoid having to walk by them. Who controlled the situation? The other person did. As long as you are controlled by the past behavior of another person, you aren't free. That person and what they did is controlling you.

When you refuse to offer or receive forgiveness, you remain tied to that person or that event for the rest of your life. Think about this. If you are refusing to forgive someone because you want them to hurt the way you hurt, you are at least as bad as they are. You may actually be worse. They may have hurt you unintentionally, but you are trying to hurt them intentionally. Is that who you want to be? Is that how you want to live your life? You could be free and making decisions that make you happy and successful, but you can't because you are preoccupied with making someone else suffer because you suffered. You have become the villain in your own life story.

If you want to regain the power and control over your life, offering and receiving forgiveness is the path that will take you there.

If you have discovered a new interest and openness to forgiveness, you may be ready to enter the next stage.

STAGE 2: FINDING THE ABILITY TO FORGIVE

In stage 2, you may feel like, *I would like to be able to forgive them, but I don't think I can.* That's good. That's progress. Now we can ask the question, "What is forgiveness?"

First of all, forgiveness is a transaction. We use the term all the time in a business sense. A loan can be forgiven. A debt can be forgiven. When someone has hurt or injured us, we feel we are justified in thinking they owe us something in return. Forgiveness is the release of that debt or obligation. It's getting to the point where you don't want or need anything from the other person.

Suppose a friend asks you to borrow a thousand dollars. This is a good friend, and you happen to have a thousand dollars to lend, so you say, "Sure, I'll lend you a thousand dollars. Pay me back when you can." Your friend says, "Thank you so much! I'll pay you back as soon as I get paid." Then payday comes, and the friend doesn't pay you back. It was a rough week, and your friend had some unexpected expenses. The paycheck was short. Whatever. But this is a good friend, so you say, "No problem, pay me back when you can." Then a week becomes a month. One month becomes several months, and the relationship is starting to get weird. At first, your friend kept making excuses by saying, "Next paycheck, I promise." Then they started getting scarce. Now, you never see them, and it's almost like they are avoiding you and not taking your calls. But this is a very good friend. You decide this friendship is worth more to you than a thousand dollars. You call the friend and say, "Hey, don't worry about that thousand dollars. Consider it a gift. I'm letting it go. Your friendship is worth more to me than a thousand dollars. I'm not going to let that come between us." That's forgiveness. It's letting something go. You take the debt out of the books and release the other person from any obligation. You move to the place where they don't owe you anything.

But if you forgive somebody, it is going to cost you something. Forgiving always costs the one who is doing the forgiving. When you forgive someone a $1,000 debt, it costs you $1,000. The person who is doing the forgiving has to pick up the tab and live with the consequences of the other person's behavior.

Why would you choose to do that? Because the value of forgiving is greater than the cost of forgiving. You can begin to appreciate the value of forgiveness by asking yourself five questions.

1. Who do I need to forgive?

2. Why do I need to forgive them?

3. What will it cost me to forgive them?

4. What do I have to give up in order to forgive them?

5. How will my life get better if I forgive them?

As you work through these questions, forgiveness will make more sense, and it will increase in value, even while you are counting the cost.

STAGE 3: FINDING THE REALITY OF FORGIVENESS

Most people don't realize forgiveness is a skill, and it takes practice. The more you do it, the better you get at it. The reality of forgiveness is that it happens over time. Yes, it's a decision you make in a moment, but experiencing the reality of that decision and feeling the effects of that decision takes time. You may think you have forgiven the person, but then you say, do, or feel something that lets you know you're not as far along in the process as you thought you were.

The good news is that the pain gets less over time. When you enter the process of forgiveness, it still hurts. A lot. And that pain doesn't go away immediately, but over time, it hurts less. At first, it hurts too much to talk or think about. Then, it hurts less to talk and think about it. Soon, it doesn't hurt at all to talk or think about it. Eventually, you stop talking and thinking about it unless there's a reason to. You start going longer periods of time without thinking about it. It's still part of who you are. You still have the memories, but it becomes less significant and relevant to your daily life.

Forgiveness is a skill, and like any skill, it takes time and practice to get good at it. The more often you do it and the longer you do it, the better you get at it.

STAGE 4: FINDING YOUR OWN FORGIVENESS

When people tell me they are struggling with forgiving themselves, the first thing I usually tell them is this.

"Don't kick your own ass."

It's not very professional or polite, but it's memorable. Here's the point. There's no value in beating yourself up over past mistakes. As Patty Loveless sang, "You can feel bad if it makes you feel better." But it doesn't benefit anyone else, and it doesn't make anything better.

Don't worry. If you have an ass kicking coming, life will provide it. The Bible says, "Don't be fooled, A person will reap what they sow." Karma says, "What goes around, comes around." It's like in the movies when someone is reunited with an old flame. (Think Capt. Jack Sparrow, Indiana Jones, etc.) They get slapped and respond with, "Yeah, I deserved that one." When we've wronged people, when we've hurt and disappointed people in the past, some of that is going to catch up with us. We will experience consequences from past mistakes and behaviors, and that's okay. When we get what we deserve, it's called justice, and justice is a good thing. Justice is fair. We accept justice and learn to live with it.

But what happens when we don't get justice? What happens when we get grace? Or mercy? What happens when, as Dave

Ramsey puts it, we're doing better than we deserve? How can we receive good things in life when we know we've done lots of bad things? *That's* not fair.

It can be very difficult to take the forgiveness practices and principles we give to others and apply them to ourselves. Why?

Forgiving ourselves takes a lot of humility, but refusing to forgive ourselves is actually arrogant, self-centered, and indicates a lack of humility. When we forgive others but don't forgive ourselves, we are saying, "I can forgive you but not myself because I'm worse than you."

Forgiving yourself can also anger people who haven't forgiven you yet. When someone feels like you deserve to be punished and you refuse to punish yourself, they may feel the need to punish you. That's on them. You may have to accept it, but that doesn't mean you have to punish yourself to satisfy someone else's sense of justice.

If you are a spiritual person, you may also have trouble accepting forgiveness from God, the Universe, or your higher power. That is a separate issue from forgiving yourself. I recommend you seek out a spiritual community and a spiritual advisor to seek their support in resolving that issue.

When trying to forgive yourself, I recommend you use the same questions you would use in working through your forgiveness of others.

1. WHO DO I NEED TO FORGIVE?

That would be me.

2. WHY DO I NEED TO FORGIVE MYSELF?

You may look inside and come to the conclusion that there's really nothing to forgive. You've done your best. Things happen. You struggle, but all things considered, you did the best you could under difficult circumstances. Yes, you made some mistakes and maybe some bad decisions, but everybody does that. That doesn't make you a bad person; it only makes you human.

Are you trying to forgive yourself for failing? Okay. Forgive yourself. Everybody fails. Failing does not make you a failure. During March Madness, sixty-four very good college basketball teams make the bracket. How many of them lose their final game? Sixty-three. On any given Sunday, half of all professional football teams *lose*. Nobody succeeds all the time at everything. You are allowed to fail. The trick is to learn to fail well.

Are you trying to forgive yourself for disappointing yourself or someone else? Handling disappointment is all about managing expectations. To put the question another way, "What did you expect?" Were those expectations realistic? Were they justified? Why did you expect that? Life is full of disappointments. We disappoint ourselves and others. Others disappointment us. It's okay to forgive yourself for that.

Are you trying to forgive yourself for hurting someone? That one is hard, especially if you hurt someone you care about or someone who cares about you. You probably didn't mean to. Or maybe you did. Either way, this one is going to take some work. You are going to have to work the CRAFT restoration process hard. But remember, hurting yourself doesn't take the hurt from someone else. Punishing yourself doesn't take away the pain from someone else. If you want to find atonement or redemption, you will have to give yourself the forgiveness you want to receive from the other person *first*.

3. WHAT WILL IT COST ME TO FORGIVE MYSELF?

Think about it. If you forgive yourself, you will be giving up your excuses for not doing good, for not succeeding, or accomplishing anything useful. That's right. If you forgive yourself and take responsibility for your behavior, you are going to have to get back into your life and start living well and doing good. It's easier to sit back, blame yourself, make excuses, and do nothing. But in the words of Dr. Phil, "How's that working for you?"

4. WHAT DO I LOSE OR HAVE TO GIVE UP IN ORDER TO FORGIVE MYSELF?

Pride. Yes. That's right. If you are sitting there thinking, *I can't forgive myself because I'm the worst person who's ever lived, and I don't deserve forgiveness,* then you are still being self-absorbed and self-centered. Yes, it is about you, but it's not *all* about you. Get over yourself. Let it go. Go on living and try to do some good along the way.

5. HOW WILL MY LIFE GET BETTER IF I FORGIVE MYSELF?

You will be free to succeed or fail, try new things, live, accept whatever love and happiness life may bring you, and find meaning and purpose and maybe some redemption. How will your life be better if you don't forgive yourself? It won't be. You can continue to wallow in remorse and regret if you want, but that won't change the past, will it? That won't make anything better, will it? Forgive yourself and move on. I know, it's easier said than done, but most things in life are. If you need some help, ask for it. Talk to somebody. It's worth it. You're worth it.

PART V

Your Family
Action Plan

16

FAMILY VALUES

*"Values are statements about what we want to be doing with
our life: about what we want to stand for. And how we want
to behave on an ongoing basis. They are leading principles that
can guide us and motivate us as we move through life."*

—ACT Made Simple

The supportive family is guided by values. You, individually, are guided by values. You have gotten to this chapter in this book because you have been fueled and guided by your values. There is something important to you, something you want, and you believe continuing to read this book is going to help you get it. I believe you are right. You've read to this point in the book because having a supportive family is one of your values.

HOW FAMILY VALUES ARE FORMED

When thinking about family values, it's helpful to think in triangles. Family values are formed in triangles. Here's what I mean. You have a set of values. They were formed over the course of your lifetime, and they were heavily influenced by your family. Your individual values are a result of a set of values that were formed by the relationship between two other people—your parents. They each had their own individual values they brought to the relationship. Some of those values were shared, some were not. Simply put, Mom has a set of values, and Dad has a set of values. Mom and Dad have a set of shared values. You pick and choose from the values of your mom and dad, add a few you pick up from other influences, and develop your own set of values. Three people. Triangles.

Here's a summary of how individual values are formulated.

"Your individual values are rooted in your birth family, developed in your growth family, and expressed in your life family."

Let's unpack that.

FAMILY VALUES ARE ROOTED IN YOUR BIRTH FAMILY

You were born into a family context that had a set of values (see Chapter 3). Your birth parents were influenced by their parents, who were influenced by their parents, and back it goes. This produces an accumulation of values over time. Your parents took the heritage of values they were raised with and sorted through them. They kept and embraced some of those values. They modified some and out-right rejected some others. This helped them produce their own individual value systems, which influenced the decisions they made, which resulted in you being born.

Here's an example. As I am writing this chapter, the nation is mourning the death of President George H.W. Bush (41). He is being honored for his character and service, and he is also being recognized as a family man. People are discussing his legacy, but it raises the question, "What was his father like?"

George H.W. Bush was a descendant of Prescott Bush, who graduated from Yale. He was descended from Rev. James

Smith Bush, who also graduated from Yale. Do you want to guess where George 41 graduated from? If you are born into a family where your father and grandfather both graduated from Yale, you have inherited a set of values.

Compare that to the heritage of another recent president, Jimmy Carter (39). Was he raised as a humble peanut farmer? Well, not exactly. He was "raised in a wealthy family of peanut farmers in the southern town of Plains in Georgia."[1]

His roots in America go back to the 1700s when his first ancestor came to America.

Andrew Seawright was born about 1712 in Ireland. He and his family immigrated to South Carolina, arriving in Charleston in 1762. Among the family traveling with him was his son James Seawright, 4th great-grandfather of President Carter. James Seawright would meet his wife Elizabeth McCullough, 4th great-grandmother of President Carter, aboard the ship from Ireland.

President Jimmy Carter has a number of fellow U. S. Presidents among his famous kin. This includes, but is not limited to, Zachary Taylor, William H. Harrison, Benjamin Harrison, Theodore Roosevelt, George Washington, Richard Nixon, and Barack Obama. He also has royal connections that include being a direct descendant of King Edward I and to the current royal family through kinship to Princess Diana and Catherine Middleton.[2]

There's an older example I'd like to share from one of the earliest studies of American Education. Illustrating the priority Jonathan and Sarah Edwards placed on training their children, A.E. Winship's *Jukes-Edwards: A Study in Education and Heredity* revealed that Edwards' descendants included:

1 U.S. Vice-President,
3 U.S. Senators,
3 governors,

3 mayors,
13 college presidents,
30 judges,
65 professors,
80 public office holders,
100 lawyers, and
100 missionaries.

This same study examined a family known as Jukes.

In 1877, while visiting New York's prisons, Richard Dugdale found inmates with forty-two different last names all descending from one man, called Max. Born around 1720 of Dutch stock, Max was a hard drinker, idle, irreverent, and uneducated.

Max's descendants included:

7 murderers,
60 thieves,
50 women of debauchery,
130 other convicts;
310 paupers, who, when combined, spent 2,300 years in poorhouses, and
400 physically wrecked by indulgent living.

The Jukes descendants cost the state more than $1,250,000.[3]

What do we learn from all this? Often when teenagers are angry, depressed, disappointed, or not getting their way, they will use their history or their parent's history as a weapon or a negotiating tool. It's called manipulation, and kids are good at it. When the sentence comes out, it sounds something like this. "I didn't ask to be born." Boom. There it is. The definitive argument, the mic drop moment.

Or is it? I responded, "You are right. You didn't ask to be born. Nobody does. That's not how it works. As far as we know, there's not a room of pre-existent souls waiting to be assigned parents. And even if there were, when the person in charge says, "Hey, I got a pair of crappy parents in a rotten family that need a kid," nobody says, "Ooh, pick me, I'll go." Yeah, you didn't get perfect parents. Guess what? They didn't get a perfect kid. It may not be your fault, but now it's your responsibility to deal with it. You can be crushed by the weight of your family history, or you can get on top of it and build something new." Sometimes the kids didn't like me very much.

FAMILY HISTORY AND EPIGENETICS

Epigenetics is a relatively new field of study in psychology and neuroscience. It looks at how traumatic experiences are stored in the body and passed on to future generations.

> Here's an analogy that might further help you to understand what epigenetics is, as presented in Nessa Carey's *Epigenetics Revolution*. Think of the human lifespan as a very long movie. The cells would be the actors and actresses, essential units that make up the movie. DNA, in turn, would be the script — instructions for all the participants of the movie to perform their roles. Subsequently, the DNA sequence would be the words on the script, and certain blocks of these words that instruct key actions or events to take place would be the genes. The concept of genetics would be like screenwriting. Follow the analogy so far? Great. The concept of *epi*-genetics, then, would be like directing. The script can be the same, but the director can choose to eliminate or tweak certain scenes or dialogue, altering the movie for better or worse. After all, Steven Spielberg's finished product would be drastically different than Woody Allen's for the same movie script, wouldn't it?[4]

But didn't we establish in Chapter 4 that people are free to do what they wish with their family heritage? Yes, we did. You can change your family tree in one branch. One scientist described it this way. "The genome has long been known as the blueprint of life, but the epigenome is life's Etch A

Sketch: Shake it hard enough, and you can wipe clean the family curse."[5]

The point is this. You have roots, so you had to come from somewhere. And your roots and heritage affect you in ways you may not even know about. It's where you come from, but it doesn't have to be where you are going. Your family history and genetics are descriptive, not definitive. You were dealt a hand of cards at birth, and you have to play them. How you play them is up to you.

FAMILY VALUES ARE DEVELOPED IN YOUR GROWTH FAMILY

The values you function with were highly influenced by your growth family. Your parent or parents had a set of values that controlled their behavior and created the family environment you grew up with. Everything from the jobs they had to the house where they lived, how it was decorated, and the number of siblings you have are results of those values.

As you grew up, you became aware of these values. In your childhood years, you assumed they were normal. You thought they were right, true and good, and society shared them because your family is your first exposure to society. As you got older, you learned other families and other groups and organizations had other values. You started to understand you had some options and could make some choices when it came to values. You began your own process of sorting values. You compared and contrasted the values of your growth family with other sets of values. You embraced some of the values you were raised with and rejected some of them, exactly as your parents had done with their families.

> SUPPORTIVE FAMILIES SUPPORT OTHER FAMILIES.

As a result, you arrived at adulthood with a set of individual values influenced by your birth family and developed in your growth family but not identical to the values of either of them. In fact, even siblings who share biological parents can end up with wildly different sets of individual values, depending on how they sorted their family values. Differences in personality and life experiences can cause siblings to have very different criteria for sorting their growth family's values. A more compliant child can embrace a greater percentage of the growth family's values while a strong-willed oppositional child can reject most of their growth family's values. And the fun part is those siblings can switch positions as adults.

How does our relationship with our growth family values change over time? Here's my first attempt at a theory. (For a discussion on Prov. 22:6, the "train up a child" verse, see chapter 4.)

I don't know that we tend to move from rejecting to embracing more growth family values as we get older. I think what happens is the growth family values we embrace become more important to us, and we hold onto them more tightly as we grow older.

FAMILY VALUES ARE EXPRESSED IN YOUR LIFE FAMILY

In building your life family, the family you choose to share your life with, you want to surround yourself with people who share and support your values. They may be relatives, friends, neighbors, or co-workers. But it is important that they support you in living out the values you have.

The first time I remember ever seeing my dad cry was at a polka festival but not for the reason you might think. Polka music is one of our shared family values.

Polka music was part of the environment my dad was raised in. But that environment also included a lot of negative influences like alcoholism, anger, depression, and abuse. To create a better life for him and his family, he rejected that environment and those values. He and my mom moved far away from those influences and created a new family culture that rejected all those things. My upbringing was marked by sobriety, stability, and religion. Not that those negative traits were entirely absent from my family, but they were forced into the background, and I am a better person for it.

But that day at the polka festival, with a tear in his eye, Dad looked at me and said, "Maybe we gave up too much." He was confessing that maybe in trying to shield his family from the negative influences of their youth, my parents had let go of some positive values as well. Here's the principle they understood.

"You can change your values, but you can't compromise the ones you have."

In fact, the ability to change your values is a mark of maturity and wisdom. Do you have exactly the same values you had when you were younger? Probably not. With time, age, and experience, we refine our sense of what matters and what doesn't. Mental health occurs when we live consistently with our values. Spiritual health occurs when find the faith that gives us guidance for daily life.

PROFESSED VALUES VS. PRACTICAL VALUES

Your professed values are the values you state, the values you talk about. Your practical values are the values you live. If you want to see what your practical values are, look at how you spend your time, energy, and money. When it comes to families, children tend to pick up your practical values, not your professed values. They tend to model who you are and what they see, not who you want to be and what you say. The goal of family values is to make the professed values and the practical values as close as possible..

INDIVIDUAL VALUES VS. FAMILY VALUES

Family values are not a predetermined set of values. It is a recognition of the values you share as a family. Your family values are not the individual values you hold but the values shared by the family. There's the conflict. Children also have the ability to accept or reject the values of the parent.
Think in terms of our overlapping relational circles.

You have your values. They have their values, We have our values. I have long theorized that perfect couples consist of two people with contrasting personalities, but similar values. At least that's part of what has kept Lorrie and I together all these years. Conflicting values can be a source of family friction. Shared values can be a source of structure and stability.

17

FAMILY MISSION

It was only in the process of writing this book that I recognized this last principle regarding families. Looking back, family missions was a distinctive trait in my growth family, and it is a trait that makes me proud when I see it in my children. The principle is this:

Some may know it as *nobless oblige,* which is "the inferred responsibility of privileged people to act with generosity and nobility toward those less privileged."[1]

The way I learned it was on a bumper sticker I saw driving down the Schuylkill Expressway while doing inner-city work in Philadelphia. Obviously, it made an impression. The bumper sticker said, "Those of us who have been fortunate have an obligation to help those who have not."

It's also called sharing. The idea is that we don't hoard the blessings of a supportive family and keep them to ourselves. We share the blessings with those we meet who are not fortunate enough to have a supportive family of their own. Whether we make them part of our family or not is a matter of choice and boundaries.

When a family is supportive, each of the members of the family benefit and become more productive than they could have been on their own. That enhanced productivity produces resources that cover the needs of the family and usually create a surplus. The surplus can be shared with others. In Financial Peace University, Dave Ramsey emphasizes that one of the best parts of having your finances under control is the experience of being able to help others

The thing about sharing resources as a family is that when done wisely, it enhances the overall quality of relationships within the family. This book is a resource that comes from the surplus goodness I have experienced in my family. It is my hope that it helps others, and it is also my hope that it helps my own family in the process.

In formulating a family mission, we are going to look at three connections.

1) CONNECT TO YOUR FAMILY VALUES

Your family mission should follow your family values. What you do to help others should flow out of what you care about. A large part of the values of my growth family centered around faith and music, which then became an avenue for helping others.

2) CONNECT ACROSS GENERATIONAL LINES

As you may remember from Chapter 1, I am a very strong proponent of multigenerational activities, and I believe that intergenerationalism is an essential part of what it means to be a family. Because of that, I suggest that as you begin to plan your family mission projects, you make them multigenerational on purpose. Include at least two generations, three if possible. Older and younger people make great volunteers, and each has the ability to benefit the other.

Respect for Elders

We should respect and care for those who are older because we are all getting older.

Being involved in a mission is significant for the elderly because it helps them maintain some sense of meaning and purpose in their lives. A variety of necessary tasks at the hospital where I work are performed by older volunteers.

Nurturing of Children

Children learn to care for others by example. I have a recording of my father playing "How Great Thou Art" on an accordion at a nursing home while my sister sings along. In the background, you can hear one of the residents singing along loudly and off-key. It's beautiful. I can't remember how many times we visited nursing homes as a family. Now my daughter manages one. Coincidence? I don't think so.

3) CONNECT TO A LARGER COMMUNITY

Natural Communities

When planning service activities, it is easy to think of participating as part of a natural community. Natural communities are communities that form, well, naturally. They come together around something shared. Natural communities follow the principle that like attracts like and birds of a feather flock together. They can also be called affinity groups because they are formed around a common attraction. In one way or another, they are made up of people like yourself. There are strengths and values of natural communities. We all want to be a part of a community of people who are in some ways like ourselves. We get many of the family essentials, especially a sense of belonging, from natural communities. Involvement in a natural community is good and beneficial

Purposeful Community

Purposeful communities are a bit different because they stand in contrast to natural communities. They are made up of people not like me. In a day of amplified sectarianism and partisanship, we need to connect ourselves to communities of people who are not like us, people we wouldn't naturally associate with.

My parents had a good understanding of this. In Lancaster County, PA, in the late sixties and early seventies, there was a program called Fresh Air. It brought people from poor sections of New York City together with people in rural areas of Pennsylvania. My parents got involved in the program and allowed us children to meet people who were, in many ways, not like us. Not only did the inner-city kids come to visit and stay with our family, but my parents also took the initiative, and we went to New York City to visit and stay with their families.

The reason two of my children were born in Philadelphia was because my wife and I went to do church ministry with people who were not like us. This is a family value that was passed on from my parents to me. I believe it is valuable to connect your family to people who are not like them. It broadens their horizons and perspectives, and it also teaches and models inclusion and diversity. If there's not enough diversity in your own family, connect with another family that is diverse. Do it on purpose and make it work.

So, who should you help? Start with your neighbor. But who is my neighbor? Somebody once asked Jesus that question, and he answered it by telling the story of the Good Samaritan. We used to have a hospital by that name in my town, but it was recently closed by their corporate health network owners. Here's the story. I share it in the hope that we end up with more Good Samaritans and fewer corporate health networks.

The Parable of the Good Samaritan (Luke 10:25-37 NIV)

On one occasion, an expert in the law stood up to test Jesus. "Teacher," he asked, "what must I do to inherit eternal life?"

"What is written in the Law?" he replied. "How do you read it?"

He answered, "Love the Lord your God with all your heart and with all your soul and with all your strength and with all your mind; and Love your neighbor as yourself.

"You have answered correctly," Jesus replied. "Do this, and you will live."

But he wanted to justify himself, so he asked Jesus, "And who is my neighbor?"

In reply Jesus said, "A man was going down from Jerusalem to Jericho when he was attacked by robbers. They stripped him of his clothes, beat him, and went away, leaving him half-dead. A priest happened to be going down the same road, and when he saw the man, he passed by on the other side. So, too, a Levite, when he came to the place and saw him, passed by on the other side. But a Samaritan, as he traveled, came where the man was; and when he saw him, he took pity on him. He went to him and bandaged his wounds, pouring on oil and wine. Then he put the man on his own donkey, brought him to an inn, and took care of him. The next day, he took out two denarii and gave them to the innkeeper. "Look after him," he said, "and when I return, I will reimburse you for any extra expense you may have."

"Which of these three do you think was a neighbor to the man who fell into the hands of robbers?"

The expert in the law replied, "The one who had mercy on him."

Jesus told him, "Go and do likewise."

The point of the story is simple and obvious. When you see someone in need and you have the resources to help that person, you do it. You can't help everyone, but you can help someone. Helping others as a family will add a significant spiritual dimension to your family. And who knows? Maybe if you show your children how to care for others, they may someday be willing to help care for you.

18

NEXT STEPS

The purpose of this book is to empower and equip you to build a strong, healthy, supportive family out of the people you already have in your life. Hopefully, we have succeeded in doing so. Now, it's time to get started. As they say in recovery programs, do the next right thing. As they say in ACT programs, it's time to ... well ... act.

TAKE THE FIRST STEPS FROM PART I

Remember, to have a strong, healthy, supportive family, you must be willing to become a strong, healthy, supportive person. This has been a book about families, but it is also a self-help book. It's not a book about getting other people to change; it's a book about changing how we relate to other people.

Create a list of the people in your life who give you the five essentials listed in Chapter Two.

Create a to do list of things you can do to make the relationships with these people stronger, healthier, and more supportive.

Create a list of people you respect and make the time to build stronger relationships with them.

Be sure to include multiple generations in your list. We want to give and receive support from people who are older and younger than us.

START BUILDING—PART II

Remember, the basic principles of building a family are show up, listen up, speak up, and grow up.

Show Up

Who are the people in your life who need you to show up?

What can you do to manage your time differently and create time to be more available?

Listen Up

Who has been trying to tell you something important, and you've been arguing instead of listening?

Speak Up

What is one important conversation you need to have to set boundaries?

What is one important conversation you need to have where you need to get something out that you've been holding inside?

Grow Up

What is one area where you need to grow up and behave more like an adult and less like a child?

REDUCE FRICTION—PART III

Who in your family do you experience the most friction with?

How can you apply FFRP to this relationship? (Look inside. Listen to understand. Love unconditionally. Let go and hold on.)

START HEALING—PART IV

What is the family pain you need to accept and quit trying to avoid?

What stage are you at with your emotional healing?

What relationship do you want to attempt to restore using the CRAFT process?

Who do you need to forgive? Where are you at with the process?

START LIVING—PART V

What are your personal values that give life meaning and purpose?

What are the values you share with your family?

Who are you most able to help with the support of your family?

ENDNOTES

INTRODUCTION

[1] Pew Research Center analysis of 1960-2014 Decennial Census and 2010 and 2014 American Community Survey.. Published in Per Social Trends. 12/17/2015 www.pewsocialtrends.org

[2] Gross, Dr. Gail, <u>A Stable Home Equals a Successful Child.</u> HuffPost Life 4/15, 2017

CHAPTER 1

[1] Rosenberg. (<u>https://www.thoughtco.com/names-of-generations-1435472</u>)

[2] <u>https://www.youtube.com/watch?v=IQuc7wfO16Q</u>

[3]<u>https://news.uchicago.edu/story/meeting-online-leads-happier-more-enduring-marriages</u>

Chapter 2

[1] Hagerty, et al. "Sense of Belonging: A Vital Mental Health Concept." Archives of Psychiatric Nursing, Vol VI, No. 3 (June) 1992: pp. 172-177

[2] by Stephen Schwarz

Chapter 3

[1] Walcheski et al., Family Life Education: The Practice of Family Science NCFR 2015. P.172-173

[2] https://www.uscis.gov/citizenship/learners/citizenship-rights-and-responsibilities

[3] Kimberly A. Powell, Tamara D. Afifi, "Uncertainty Management and Adoptees' Ambiguous Loss of Their Birth Parents," *Journal of Social and Personal Relationships*, 22 (2005): 129-151.

Chapter 12

[1] https://www.integrativepainscienceinstitute.com/acceptance-and-commitment-therapy-act-for-chronic-pain/

[2] *Songwriters: Daniel Wayne Sermon / Daniel Coulter Reynolds / Benjamin Arthur McKee / Daniel James Platzman / Robin Lennart Fredriksson / Mattias Per Larsson / Justin Drew Tranter*

Chapter 16

[1] https://www.thesun.co.uk/news/7913951/jimmy-carter-us-president-health-wife-rosalynn/

[2] https://famouskin.com/family-tree.php?name=12937+-jimmy+carter

[3] https://selfeducatedamerican.com/2011/10/04/jonathan-edwards-v-max-jukes/

[4] https://www.whatisepigenetics.com/what-is-epigenetics/
[5] http://discovermagazine.com/2013/may/13-grand-mas-experiences-leave-epigenetic-mark-on-your-genes

CHAPTER 17

[1] https://www.google.com/search?q=noblesse+oblige&o-q=noblesse&aqs=chrome.1.69i57j0l5.5706j0j4&-sourceid=chrome&ie=UTF-8